The Cookie Bible

Publications International, Ltd.

Pictured on the front cover: Oatmeal-Chip Crispies *(page 116)*.

Pictured on the back cover *(clockwise from top left):* Apricot Almond Bars *(page 190),* Chocolate Cashew Coconut Bars *(page 198)* and Chocolate Chunk Cookies *(page 34)*.

ISBN-13: 978-1-4508-6803-7
ISBN-10: 1-4508-6803-7

Library of Congress Control Number: 2011937534

Manufactured in China.

8 7 6 5 4 3 2 1

Microwave Cooking: Microwave ovens vary in wattage. Use the cooking times as guidelines and check for doneness before adding more time.

Preparation/Cooking Times: Preparation times are based on the approximate amount of time required to assemble the recipe before cooking, baking, chilling or serving. These times include preparation steps such as measuring, chopping and mixing. The fact that some preparations and cooking can be done simultaneously is taken into account. Preparation of optional ingredients and serving suggestions is not included.

Table of Contents

Cookie Jar Classics

One-Bite Chocolate Chip Cookies
Makes about 14 dozen cookies

1¼ cups all-purpose flour
½ teaspoon baking soda
¼ teaspoon salt
½ cup packed light brown sugar
½ cup (1 stick) butter, softened

¼ cup granulated sugar
1 egg
1 teaspoon vanilla
1¼ cups mini semisweet chocolate chips
Sea salt (optional)

1. Preheat oven to 350°F.

2. Whisk flour, baking soda and salt in medium bowl. Beat brown sugar, butter and granulated sugar in large bowl with electric mixer at medium speed until light and fluffy. Beat in egg and vanilla until blended. Add flour mixture; beat at low speed until well blended. Stir in chocolate chips.

3. Drop dough by ½ teaspoonfuls 1 inch apart onto ungreased cookie sheets. Sprinkle very lightly with sea salt, if desired.

4. Bake 6 minutes or just until edges are lightly browned. (Centers of cookies will be very light and will not look done.) Cool on cookie sheets 2 minutes. Remove to wire racks; cool completely.

Butter Pecan Crisps

Makes about 5 dozen cookies

1 cup (2 sticks) unsalted butter, softened
¾ cup granulated sugar
¾ cup packed brown sugar
½ teaspoon salt
2 eggs
1½ cups finely ground pecans
1 teaspoon vanilla

2½ cups sifted all-purpose flour
1 teaspoon baking soda
30 pecan halves
4 squares (1 ounce each) semisweet chocolate
1 tablespoon shortening

1. Preheat oven to 375°F. Line cookie sheets with parchment paper.

2. Beat butter, granulated sugar, brown sugar and salt in large bowl with electric mixer at medium speed until light and fluffy. Add eggs, one at a time, beating well after each addition. Beat in ground pecans and vanilla. Combine flour and baking soda in small bowl. Gradually add flour mixture to butter mixture, beating well after each addition.

3. Spoon dough into large pastry bag fitted with ⅜-inch round tip; fill bag halfway. Shake down dough to remove air bubbles. Hold bag about ½ inch above prepared cookie sheets. Pipe dough into 1¼-inch balls, spacing 3 inches apart. Cut each pecan half lengthwise into 2 slivers. Press 1 sliver in center of each ball.

4. Bake 10 minutes or until lightly browned. Cool on cookie sheets 5 minutes. Remove to wire racks; cool completely.

5. Melt chocolate and shortening in small heavy saucepan over low heat; stir until blended. Drizzle chocolate mixture over cookies. Let stand until set.

Butter Pecan Crisps

Lemon Poppy Seed Cookies

Makes 2 dozen cookies

1 cup sugar

½ cup (1 stick) unsalted butter, softened

1 egg

2 tablespoons grated lemon peel

2 tablespoons poppy seeds

¼ teaspoon vanilla

1¾ cups all-purpose flour

¼ teaspoon salt

1. Beat sugar and butter in medium bowl with electric mixer at medium speed until light and fluffy. Beat in egg, lemon peel, poppy seeds and vanilla until well blended. Add flour and salt; beat just until blended. Shape dough into disc; wrap and refrigerate 1 hour.

2. Preheat oven to 325°F. Lightly grease or line cookie sheets with parchment paper.

3. Shape dough by tablespoonfuls into 1-inch balls. Place 2 inches apart on prepared cookie sheets.

4. Bake 15 minutes or until set. Cool on cookie sheets 2 minutes. Remove to wire racks; cool completely.

Tip

Cookies that are uniform in size and shape will finish baking at the same time. To easily shape drop cookies into a uniform size, use an ice cream scoop with a release bar. The bar usually has a number on it indicating the number of scoops that can be made from one quart of ice cream. The handiest size for cookies is a #40, #50 or #80 scoop.

Lemon Poppy Seed Cookies

Tiny Peanut Butter Sandwiches

Makes 6 to 7 dozen sandwiches

1¼ cups all-purpose flour
½ teaspoon baking powder
½ teaspoon baking soda
¼ teaspoon salt
½ cup granulated sugar
½ cup packed brown sugar

½ cup (1 stick) butter, softened
½ cup creamy peanut butter
1 egg
1 teaspoon vanilla
1 cup semisweet chocolate chips
½ cup whipping cream

1. Preheat oven to 350°F.

2. Whisk flour, baking powder, baking soda and salt in medium bowl. Beat granulated sugar, brown sugar and butter in large bowl with electric mixer at medium speed until light and fluffy. Beat in peanut butter, egg and vanilla until well blended. Gradually add flour mixture, beating at low speed until blended.

3. Shape dough by ½ teaspoonfuls into balls; place 1 inch apart on ungreased cookie sheets. Flatten balls slightly in crisscross pattern with tines of fork.

4. Bake 6 minutes or until set. Cool on cookie sheets 4 minutes. Remove to wire racks; cool completely.

5. Meanwhile, place chocolate chips in medium heatproof bowl. Place cream in small microwavable bowl. Microwave on HIGH 2 minutes or just until simmering; pour over chocolate chips. Let stand 2 minutes; stir until smooth. Let stand 10 minutes or until filling thickens to desired consistency.

6. Spread scant teaspoonful of filling on flat sides of half of cookies; top with remaining cookies.

Tiny Peanut Butter Sandwiches

Oatmeal Macaroons
Makes 4 dozen cookies

1 cup (2 sticks) margarine or butter, softened

1 cup firmly packed brown sugar

2 eggs

½ teaspoon almond extract

1¼ cups all-purpose flour

1 teaspoon baking soda

3 cups QUAKER® Oats (quick or old fashioned uncooked)

1 package (4 ounces) flaked or shredded coconut (about 1⅓ cups)

1. Heat oven to 350°F. Lightly grease cookie sheets.

2. Beat margarine and brown sugar in large bowl with electric mixer until creamy. Add eggs and almond extract; beat well. Add combined flour and baking soda; mix well. Add oats and coconut; mix well.

3. Drop dough by rounded teaspoonfuls onto prepared cookie sheets.

4. Bake 8 to 10 minutes or until light golden brown. Cool 2 minutes on cookie sheets; remove to wire racks. Cool completely. Store tightly covered.

Cinnamon-Sugar Knots
Makes about 4 dozen cookies

¼ cup sugar

¾ teaspoon ground cinnamon

1 package (about 18 ounces) spice cake mix

1 package (8 ounces) cream cheese, softened

1. Preheat oven to 350°F. Combine sugar and cinnamon in small bowl.

2. Beat cake mix and cream cheese in large bowl with electric mixer at medium speed until well blended. Shape dough by tablespoonfuls into 1-inch balls; roll each ball into log about 4 inches long. Gently coil dough and pull up ends to form knot. Place 1½ inches apart on ungreased cookie sheets. Sprinkle with cinnamon-sugar mixture.

3. Bake 10 minutes or until edges are lightly browned. Cool on cookie sheets 2 minutes. Remove to wire racks; cool completely.

Oatmeal Macaroons

Mexican Sugar Cookies

Makes about 5 dozen cookies

2½ cups (2½ sticks) shortening
2 cups sugar, divided
1 teaspoon ground anise
2 eggs
¼ cup orange juice

6 cups all-purpose flour
1 tablespoon baking powder
½ teaspoon cream of tartar
½ teaspoon salt
3 tablespoons ground cinnamon

1. Beat shortening, 1 cup sugar and anise in large bowl with electric mixer at medium speed until light and fluffy. Add eggs, one at a time, beating well after each addition. Add orange juice; beat until light and fluffy.

2. Whisk flour, baking powder, cream of tartar and salt in medium bowl. Gradually add to shortening mixture, beating well after each addition.

3. Knead dough on lightly floured surface. Shape dough into two discs; wrap and refrigerate 30 minutes.

4. Preheat oven to 350°F. Lightly grease or line cookie sheets with parchment paper. Combine remaining 1 cup sugar and cinnamon in small bowl.

5. Working with one disc at a time, roll out dough between sheets of parchment paper to ½-inch thickness. Cut out shapes with cookie cutters. Gently press dough trimmings together; reroll and cut out additional cookies. Place 2 inches apart on prepared cookie sheets.

6. Bake 8 minutes or until lightly browned. Cool on cookies sheets 2 minutes; dip cookies in cinnamon-sugar mixture. Remove to wire racks; cool completely.

Mexican Sugar Cookies

Flourless Peanut Butter Chocolate Chippers

Makes 1½ dozen cookies

1 cup packed light brown sugar
1 cup creamy or chunky peanut butter
1 egg

Granulated sugar
½ cup milk chocolate chips

1. Preheat oven to 350°F.

2. Beat brown sugar, peanut butter and egg in medium bowl with electric mixer at medium speed until well blended. Shape dough by heaping tablespoonfuls into 1½-inch balls. Place 2 inches apart on ungreased cookie sheets. Dip fork into granulated sugar; flatten each ball to ½-inch thickness, crisscrossing with fork. Press 3 to 4 chocolate chips on top of each cookie.

3. Bake 12 minutes or until set. Cool on cookie sheets 2 minutes. Remove to wire racks; cool completely.

Grape-Filled Cookies

Makes about 1 dozen cookies

2 cups coarsely chopped California
seedless grapes
¼ cup packed brown sugar

½ teaspoon ground cinnamon
1 teaspoon lemon juice
Sugar Cookie Dough (recipe follows)

Combine grapes, brown sugar and cinnamon in saucepan. Bring to a boil; cook and stir over medium heat 35 minutes or until thickened. Stir in lemon juice; cool.

Roll Sugar Cookie Dough to ⅛-inch thickness. Cut into 24 (2½-inch) circles. Place 12 circles on greased cookie sheet. Place heaping teaspoonful of grape filling on each circle, leaving ⅛-inch border around edges. Place remaining circles over filling; press edges together with fork. Cut 3 to 5 slits through top circles of dough.

Bake at 400°F 6 to 8 minutes or until lightly browned. Cool on wire rack.

Sugar Cookie Dough: Beat ⅓ cup butter or margarine and 2 tablespoons sugar until smooth. Beat in 1 egg and ½ teaspoon vanilla. Combine 1 cup all-purpose flour, ¾ teaspoon baking powder and dash salt; stir into butter mixture. Wrap and refrigerate at least 1 hour.

*Favorite recipe from **California Table Grape Commission***

Flourless Peanut Butter Chocolate Chippers

Triple Ginger Cookies

Makes 3 dozen cookies

2 cups all-purpose flour
2 teaspoons baking soda
1 teaspoon ground ginger
½ teaspoon salt
¾ cup (1½ sticks) unsalted butter
1¼ cups sugar, divided

¼ cup light molasses
1 egg
1 tablespoon finely minced fresh ginger
1 tablespoon finely minced crystallized
    ginger*

*Semisoft sugar-coated ginger slices are preferable to the small dry ginger cubes found in the supermarket spice aisle. The softer, larger slices are available at natural foods or specialty stores. If using the small dry cubes of ginger, steep the cubes in boiling hot water a few minutes to soften. Drain the cubes, then pat dry and mince.

1. Sift flour, baking soda, ground ginger and salt onto waxed paper. Melt butter in small heavy saucepan over low heat; pour into large bowl and cool slightly. Add 1 cup sugar, molasses and egg; mix well. Add flour mixture; mix well. Add fresh ginger and crystallized ginger; stir just until blended. Cover; refrigerate 1 hour.

2. Preheat oven to 375°F. Lightly grease or line cookie sheets with parchment paper.

3. Shape dough by tablespoonfuls into 1-inch balls. Roll in remaining ¼ cup sugar. Place 3 inches apart on prepared cookie sheets. (If dough is very sticky, drop by teaspoonfuls into sugar to coat.)

4. For chewy cookies, bake 7 minutes or until edges are lightly browned. For crispier cookies, bake 9 to 11 minutes. Cool on cookie sheets 1 minute. Remove to wire racks; cool completely.

Variation: Roll dough in plastic wrap to form a log. Refrigerate up to one week or freeze up to two months. To bake, bring the dough almost to room temperature. Slice dough into ¼-inch-thick slices; dip the tops in sugar. Bake as directed above.

Triple Ginger Cookies

Orange-Almond Sables
Makes about 2 dozen cookies

1½ cups powdered sugar
1 cup (2 sticks) butter, softened
1 tablespoon finely grated orange peel
1 tablespoon almond-flavored liqueur *or*
    1 teaspoon almond extract

¾ cup whole blanched almonds, toasted*
1¾ cups all-purpose flour
¼ teaspoon salt
1 egg, beaten

To toast almonds, spread in single layer on baking sheet. Bake in preheated 375°F oven 5 to 7 minutes or until golden brown, stirring frequently.

1. Preheat oven to 375°F. Beat powdered sugar and butter in large bowl with electric mixer at medium speed until light and fluffy. Beat in orange peel and liqueur.

2. Reserve 24 whole almonds. Place remaining cooled almonds in food processor or blender; process using on/off pulsing action until almonds are ground but not pasty.

3. Whisk ground almonds, flour and salt in medium bowl. Gradually add to butter mixture, beating with electric mixer at low speed until well blended after each addition.

4. Roll out dough between sheets of parchment paper to ¼-inch thickness. Cut out shapes with 2½-inch fluted or round cookie cutter. Place 2 inches apart on ungreased cookie sheets. Press one whole reserved almond in center of each shape. Lightly brush with egg.

5. Bake 10 minutes or until lightly browned. Cool on cookie sheets 1 minute. Remove to wire racks; cool completely.

Orange-Almond Sables

Chocolate Almond Cookie Bites

Makes about 3 dozen cookies

1 (8-ounce) NESTLÉ® TOLL HOUSE®
    Semi-Sweet Chocolate Baking Bar,
    broken into pieces
2 eggs
¼ teaspoon salt
¼ cup packed brown sugar

1 teaspoon vanilla extract
1 cup chopped almonds, toasted
¼ cup all-purpose flour
    Slivered or sliced almonds

PREHEAT oven to 325°F. Grease baking sheets.

MICROWAVE baking bars in medium, uncovered, microwave-safe bowl on HIGH (100%) power for 1 minute. STIR. If pieces retain some of their original shape, microwave at additional 10- to 15-second intervals, stirring just until melted.

BEAT eggs and salt in small mixer bowl on high speed for 3 minutes or until thick. Add brown sugar; beat for additional 5 minutes. Beat in melted chocolate and vanilla extract. Stir in chopped almonds and flour. Drop by rounded teaspoonful onto prepared baking sheets. Insert one almond slice into top of each cookie.

BAKE for 8 to 10 minutes or until shiny and set. Cool on baking sheet for 2 minutes; remove to wire racks to cool completely.

Chocolate Walnut Cookie Bites: Substitute 1 cup chopped toasted walnuts for almonds. Garnish cookies with walnut pieces before baking.

Prep Time: 15 minutes • **Bake Time:** 8 to 10 minutes

Chocolate Almond Cookie Bites

Browned Butter Spritz Cookies

Makes about 8 dozen cookies

1½ cups (3 sticks) unsalted butter
½ cup granulated sugar
¼ cup powdered sugar
1 egg yolk
1 teaspoon vanilla

⅛ teaspoon almond extract
2½ cups all-purpose flour
¼ cup cake flour
¼ teaspoon salt

1. Melt butter in medium heavy saucepan over medium heat until light amber, stirring frequently. Transfer butter to large bowl. Cover and refrigerate 2 hours or until solid.

2. Let browned butter stand at room temperature 15 minutes. Preheat oven to 350°F.

3. Beat browned butter, granulated sugar and powdered sugar in large bowl with electric mixer at medium speed until light and fluffy. Add egg yolk, vanilla and almond extract; beat until well blended. Whisk all-purpose flour, cake flour and salt in small bowl. Add flour mixture to butter mixture; beat until well blended.

4. Fit cookie press with desired plate (or change plates for different shapes after first batch). Fill press with dough; press dough 1 inch apart on ungreased cookie sheets.

5. Bake 10 minutes or until lightly browned. Cool on cookie sheets 5 minutes. Remove to wire racks; cool completely.

Tip: To add holiday sparkle to these delicious cookies, press red or green glacé cherry halves into the centers or sprinkle them with colored sugar or nonpareils before baking. To add more color to the cookies, tint the dough with green food coloring before pressing and pipe red icing bows on the baked and cooled cookies.

Browned Butter Spritz Cookies

Lemon Cream Cheese Cookies

Makes about 3 dozen cookies

1¾ cups all-purpose flour
½ teaspoon baking soda
½ teaspoon salt
1 cup sugar
½ cup (1 stick) butter, softened

1 package (3 ounces) cream cheese, softened
1 egg
Grated peel and juice of 1 lemon
½ cup flaked coconut, toasted*

*To toast coconut, spread evenly on ungreased cookie sheet. Toast in preheated 350°F oven 5 to 7 minutes or until light golden brown, stirring occasionally.

1. Preheat oven to 350°F.

2. Whisk flour, baking soda and salt in medium bowl. Beat sugar, butter, cream cheese and egg in large bowl with electric mixer at medium speed until light and fluffy. Add lemon peel and juice; beat until well blended.

3. Stir in flour mixture and coconut; mix well. Drop dough by rounded teaspoonfuls 2 inches apart onto ungreased cookie sheets.

4. Bake 10 minutes or until set. Cool on cookie sheets 4 minutes. Remove to wire racks; cool completely.

Tip

If you are baking several batches of cookies, you can speed things up by placing the cookies onto sheets of parchment paper ahead of time. That way they will be ready to slide right onto the cookie sheets and into the oven. Make sure that you let the cookie sheet cool before you bake another batch on the same one or the dough can melt and spread, changing the final shape and texture of the cookies.

Lemon Cream Cheese Cookies

Butter-Nut Chocolate Topped Cookies

Makes about 2½ dozen cookies

½ cup (1 stick) butter or margarine, softened
½ cup sugar
1 egg
1 teaspoon vanilla extract
1¼ cups all-purpose flour

¼ teaspoon baking soda
⅛ teaspoon salt
30 HERSHEY®S KISSES® BRAND Milk Chocolates
½ cup ground almonds, pecans or walnuts

1. Beat butter, sugar, egg and vanilla in medium bowl until well blended. Stir together flour, baking soda and salt; add to butter mixture, beating well. If necessary, refrigerate dough until firm enough to handle.

2. Remove wrappers from chocolates. Heat oven to 350°F. Shape dough into 1-inch balls; roll in ground nuts. Place on ungreased cookie sheet.

3. Bake 10 to 12 minutes or until almost no imprint remains when touched lightly in center. Remove from oven; immediately press a chocolate into center of each cookie. Carefully remove from cookie sheet to wire rack. Cool completely. Chocolate should be set before storing.

Orange Variation: Add ¾ teaspoon freshly grated orange peel to butter mixture.

Apricot Drops

Makes about 3 dozen cookies

1 package (about 18 ounces) yellow cake mix with pudding in the mix
½ cup all-purpose flour

½ cup vegetable oil
2 eggs
1 cup chopped dried apricots

1. Preheat oven to 350°F. Lightly grease or line cookie sheets with parchment paper.

2. Beat cake mix, flour, oil and eggs in large bowl with electric mixer at medium speed until well blended. Stir in apricots. Drop dough by rounded tablespoonfuls onto prepared cookie sheets.

3. Bake 8 minutes or until lightly browned. Cool on cookie sheets 1 minute. Remove to wire racks; cool completely.

Butter-Nut Chocolate Topped Cookies

Toasted Coconut Pinwheels

Makes about 3 dozen cookies

1 package (about 18 ounces) white
  cake mix
1 package (8 ounces) cream cheese,
  softened

¼ cup all-purpose flour
1 teaspoon coconut extract or vanilla
¾ cup apricot jam
1¼ cups flaked coconut, toasted*

To toast coconut, spread in single layer in heavy skillet. Cook over medium heat 1 to 2 minutes until lightly browned, stirring frequently. Remove from skillet immediately. Cool completely.

1. Beat cake mix, cream cheese, flour and coconut extract in large bowl with electric mixer at low speed until well blended. Roll out dough between sheets of parchment paper to 13×10-inch rectangle. Spread jam over dough, leaving ½-inch border. Sprinkle with toasted coconut.

2. Roll dough jelly-roll style, starting from long side. (Do not roll paper up with dough.) Wrap and freeze 2 hours or refrigerate 4 hours or overnight.

3. Preheat oven to 350°F. Lightly grease or line cookie sheets with parchment paper. Slice dough into ¼-inch-thick slices; place 1 inch apart on prepared cookie sheets.

4. Bake 12 minutes or until set. Cool on cookie sheets 3 minutes. Remove to wire racks; cool completely.

Toasted Coconut Pinwheels

Honey Spice Balls
Makes about 2½ dozen cookies

½ cup packed brown sugar
½ cup (1 stick) butter, softened
1 egg
1 tablespoon honey
1 teaspoon vanilla

2 cups all-purpose flour
½ teaspoon baking powder
½ teaspoon ground cinnamon
¼ teaspoon ground nutmeg
Quick oats

1. Preheat oven to 350°F. Lightly grease or line cookie sheets with parchment paper.

2. Beat brown sugar and butter in large bowl with electric mixer at medium speed until light and fluffy. Add egg, honey and vanilla; beat until light and fluffy. Add flour, baking powder, cinnamon and nutmeg; beat until well blended. Shape dough by tablespoonfuls into balls; roll in oats. Place 2 inches apart on prepared cookie sheets.

3. Bake 15 minutes or until cookie tops crack slightly. Cool on cookie sheets 1 minute. Remove to wire racks; cool completely.

Citrus Coolers
Makes about 4½ dozen cookies

1½ cups powdered sugar
1 package (about 18 ounces) lemon
    cake mix
1 cup (4 ounces) pecan pieces

½ cup all-purpose flour
½ cup (1 stick) butter, melted
Grated peel and juice of 1 large orange

1. Preheat oven to 375°F. Lightly grease or line cookie sheets with parchment paper. Place powdered sugar in medium shallow bowl.

2. Beat cake mix, pecans, flour, butter, orange peel and juice in large bowl with electric mixer at medium speed until well blended. Drop dough by rounded tablespoonfuls 2 inches apart onto prepared cookie sheets.

3. Bake 13 minutes or until bottoms are lightly browned. Cool on cookie sheets 3 minutes; roll in powdered sugar. Remove to wire racks; cool completely.

Honey Spice Balls

Chunkies & Chewies

Chocolate Chunk Cookies
Makes 2 dozen cookies

1⅔ cups all-purpose flour
⅓ cup CREAM OF WHEAT® Hot Cereal
    (Instant, 1-minute, 2½-minute or
    10-minute cook time), uncooked
½ teaspoon baking soda
¼ teaspoon salt
¾ cup (1½ sticks) butter, softened

½ cup packed brown sugar
⅓ cup granulated sugar
1 egg
1 teaspoon vanilla extract
1 (11.5-ounce) bag chocolate chunks
1 cup chopped pecans

1. Preheat oven to 375°F. Lightly grease cookie sheets. Blend flour, Cream of Wheat, baking soda and salt in medium bowl; set aside.

2. Beat butter and sugars in large bowl with electric mixer at medium speed until creamy. Add egg and vanilla. Beat until fluffy. Reduce speed to low. Add Cream of Wheat mixture; mix well. Stir in chocolate chunks and pecans.

3. Drop by tablespoonfuls onto prepared cookie sheets. Bake 9 to 11 minutes or until golden brown. Let stand on cookie sheets 1 minute before transferring to wire racks to cool completely.

Tip: For a colorful item to take to a school bake sale or give as a gift, replace the chocolate chunks with multicolored candy-coated chocolate.

Prep Time: 15 minutes • **Start-to-Finish Time:** 35 minutes

Ginger Raisin Cookies

Makes about 2 dozen cookies

1½ cups all-purpose flour
1 teaspoon baking soda
1 teaspoon ground ginger
1 teaspoon grated orange peel
½ teaspoon salt
½ teaspoon ground cinnamon
¾ cup granulated sugar, divided

½ cup packed brown sugar
½ cup (1 stick) butter, softened
1 egg
3 tablespoons molasses
1 teaspoon vanilla
1 cup raisins

1. Preheat oven to 375°F. Lightly grease or line cookie sheets with parchment paper.

2. Whisk flour, baking soda, ginger, orange peel, salt and cinnamon in medium bowl. Beat ½ cup granulated sugar, brown sugar and butter in large bowl with electric mixer at medium speed 2 minutes or until light and fluffy. Add egg, molasses and vanilla; beat 1 minute. Add flour mixture and raisins; stir until blended.

3. Shape dough by tablespoonfuls into 1-inch balls. Roll in remaining ¼ cup granulated sugar. Place 1½ inches apart on prepared cookie sheets.

4. Bake 10 minutes or until edges are set and centers are still slightly soft. Cool on cookie sheets 2 minutes. Remove to wire racks; cool completely.

Ginger Raisin Cookies

Granola Cookies
Makes about 3 dozen cookies

¾ cup all-purpose flour
½ teaspoon baking soda
½ teaspoon salt
½ teaspoon cinnamon
¾ cup packed brown sugar
½ cup (1 stick) butter, softened

1 egg
1 tablespoon milk
1 cup granola
¾ cup semisweet chocolate chips
¾ cup raisins

1. Preheat oven to 350°F. Lightly grease or line cookie sheets with parchment paper.

2. Whisk flour, baking soda, salt and cinnamon in small bowl. Beat brown sugar and butter in large bowl with electric mixer at medium speed until light and fluffy. Add egg and milk; beat until well blended. Add granola, chocolate chips and raisins; beat at low speed until blended. Drop dough by rounded tablespoonfuls 1½ inches apart on prepared cookie sheets.

3. Bake 10 minutes or until lightly browned. Cool on cookie sheets 2 minutes. Remove to wire racks; cool completely.

Tip
Do not grease your cookie sheets too heavily; it can cause the cookies to spread too much and overbrown on the bottom.

Granola Cookies

Cranberry Cookies

Makes about 6 dozen cookies

1 cup (2 sticks) butter
¾ cup packed brown sugar
1 package (4-serving size) vanilla instant
    pudding mix
¼ cup granulated sugar
1 teaspoon ground cinnamon

1 teaspoon vanilla
½ teaspoon ground nutmeg
2 eggs
2¼ cups all-purpose flour
1 teaspoon baking soda
1 package (9 ounces) dried cranberries

1. Preheat oven to 350°F.

2. Beat butter, brown sugar, pudding mix, granulated sugar, cinnamon, vanilla and nutmeg in large bowl with electric mixer at medium speed until light and fluffy. Add eggs, one at a time, beating well after each addition. Gradually add flour and baking soda, beating at low speed until blended.

3. Stir in cranberries. Drop dough by rounded teaspoonfuls onto ungreased cookie sheets.

4. Bake 10 minutes or until lightly browned. Cool on cookie sheets 2 minutes. Remove to wire racks; cool completely.

Cranberry Cookies

Chunky Chocolate Chip Peanut Butter Cookies

Makes about 3 dozen cookies

1¼ cups all-purpose flour
½ teaspoon baking soda
½ teaspoon salt
½ teaspoon ground cinnamon
¾ cup (1½ sticks) butter or margarine, softened
½ cup granulated sugar
½ cup packed brown sugar

½ cup creamy peanut butter
1 large egg
1 teaspoon vanilla extract
2 cups (12-ounce package) NESTLÉ® TOLL HOUSE® Semi-Sweet Chocolate Morsels
½ cup coarsely chopped peanuts

PREHEAT oven to 375°F.

COMBINE flour, baking soda, salt and cinnamon in small bowl. Beat butter, granulated sugar, brown sugar and peanut butter in large mixer bowl until creamy. Beat in egg and vanilla extract. Gradually beat in flour mixture. Stir in morsels and peanuts.

DROP dough by rounded tablespoonful onto ungreased baking sheets. Press down slightly to flatten into 2-inch circles.

BAKE for 7 to 10 minutes or until edges are set but centers are still soft. Cool on baking sheets for 4 minutes; remove to wire racks to cool completely.

Chunky Chocolate Chip Peanut Butter Cookies

New England Raisin Spice Cookies

Makes about 5 dozen cookies

1 cup packed brown sugar
½ cup (½ stick) shortening
¼ cup (½ stick) butter
⅓ cup molasses
1 egg
2¼ cups all-purpose flour
2 teaspoons baking soda

1 teaspoon salt
¾ teaspoon ground cinnamon
¼ teaspoon ground ginger
¼ teaspoon ground cloves
⅛ teaspoon ground allspice
1½ cups raisins
Granulated sugar

1. Beat brown sugar, shortening and butter in large bowl with electric mixer at medium speed until light and fluffy. Add molasses and egg; beat until blended.

2. Combine flour, baking soda, salt, cinnamon, ginger, cloves and allspice in medium bowl. Stir in raisins. Gradually add shortening mixture, stirring just until blended. Cover; refrigerate at least 2 hours.

3. Preheat oven to 350°F.

4. Shape dough by heaping tablespoonfuls into balls. Roll in granulated sugar. Place 2 inches apart on ungreased cookie sheets.

5. Bake 8 minutes or until lightly browned. Cool on cookie sheets 1 minute. Remove to wire racks; cool completely.

New England Raisin Spice Cookies

Chunky Monkey Cookies

Makes 2½ dozen cookies

2⅔ cups all-purpose flour
½ teaspoon baking soda
¼ teaspoon salt
1 cup packed light brown sugar
1 cup (2 sticks) unsalted butter, softened
½ cup granulated sugar
¾ to 1 cup mashed ripe banana*
    (1 large banana)

1 egg
½ teaspoon banana extract (optional)
1½ cups (8 ounces) coarsely chopped
    bittersweet chocolate
1 cup coarsely chopped walnuts

Do not use overripe bananas, such as those used in quick breads. The banana flesh should be creamy white, with no brown spots.

1. Preheat oven to 300°F.

2. Whisk flour, baking soda and salt in medium bowl. Beat brown sugar, butter and granulated sugar in large bowl with electric mixer at medium speed until light and fluffy. Add banana, egg and banana extract, if desired; beat just until blended. (Banana chunks should be visible.) Beat in flour mixture just until blended.

3. Fold in chocolate and walnuts. Drop dough by rounded teaspoonfuls 2 inches apart onto ungreased cookie sheets.

4. Bake 20 minutes or until edges are lightly browned. Cool on cookie sheets 2 minutes. Remove to wire racks; cool completely.

Chunky Monkey Cookies

No-Bake Noodle Cookies
Makes 2 dozen cookies

2 cups crisp chow mein noodles
⅔ cup semisweet chocolate chips
½ cup peanut butter chips

½ cup cocktail peanuts
⅓ cup raisins

Microwave Directions

1. Line cookie sheets with parchment paper.

2. Place noodles, chocolate chips, peanut butter chips, peanuts and raisins in large microwavable bowl. Microwave on HIGH 1 minute; stir. If necessary, microwave at additional 30-second intervals until chips are melted. Stir until well blended.

3. Drop noodle mixture by teaspoonfuls onto prepared cookie sheets. Refrigerate 1 hour. Store cookies between sheets of waxed paper in airtight container in refrigerator.

Jumbo 3-Chip Cookies
Makes about 2 dozen cookies

4 cups all-purpose flour
1 teaspoon baking powder
1 teaspoon baking soda
1½ cups (3 sticks) butter, softened
1¼ cups granulated sugar
1¼ cups packed brown sugar
2 large eggs
1 tablespoon vanilla extract

1 cup (6 ounces) NESTLÉ® TOLL HOUSE®
    Milk Chocolate Morsels
1 cup (6 ounces) NESTLÉ® TOLL HOUSE®
    Semi-Sweet Chocolate Morsels
½ cup NESTLÉ® TOLL HOUSE® Premier
    White Morsels
1 cup chopped nuts

PREHEAT oven to 375°F.

COMBINE flour, baking powder and baking soda in medium bowl. Beat butter, granulated sugar and brown sugar in large mixer bowl until creamy. Beat in eggs and vanilla extract. Gradually beat in flour mixture. Stir in morsels and nuts. Drop dough by level ¼-cup measure 2 inches apart onto ungreased baking sheets.

BAKE for 12 to 14 minutes or until light golden brown. Cool on baking sheets for 2 minutes; remove to wire racks to cool completely.

No-Bake Noodle Cookies

Pineapple Oatmeal Cookies
Makes about 4 dozen cookies

1 can (20 ounces) DOLE® Crushed
   Pineapple
1½ cups packed brown sugar
1 cup (½ stick) butter or margarine, softened
1 egg
3 cups old fashioned or quick cooking oats

2 cups all-purpose flour
1 teaspoon baking powder
1 teaspoon ground cinnamon
½ teaspoon salt
1 cup DOLE® Seedless or Golden Raisins
1 cup chopped almonds, toasted (optional)

• Drain pineapple well; reserve ½ cup juice.

• Beat sugar and butter until light and fluffy in large bowl. Beat in egg, crushed pineapple and reserved juice.

• Combine oats, flour, baking powder, cinnamon, salt, raisins and almonds in medium bowl. Stir into pineapple mixture.

• Drop by heaping tablespoonfuls onto greased cookie sheets. Shape with back of spoon.

• Bake at 350°F. 20 to 25 minutes or until golden. Cool on wire racks.

Prep Time: 20 minutes • **Bake Time:** 20 to 25 minutes

Pineapple Oatmeal Cookies

Soft & Chewy Chocolate Drops

Makes about 5 dozen cookies

4 squares BAKER'S® Unsweetened
    Chocolate
¾ cup (1½ sticks) butter or margarine*
2 cups sugar
3 eggs
1 teaspoon vanilla

2 cups flour
1 tub (8 ounces) COOL WHIP® Whipped
    Topping (Do not thaw.)
6 squares BAKER'S® Semi-Sweet Baking
    Chocolate

*For best results, use butter. If using margarine, add an additional ½ cup flour.

HEAT oven to 350°F. Microwave unsweetened chocolate and butter in large microwaveable bowl on HIGH 2 minutes or until butter is melted. Stir until chocolate is completely melted. Add sugar; mix well. Blend in eggs and vanilla. Add flour; mix well. Refrigerate 1 hour or until dough is easy to handle.

SHAPE dough into 1-inch balls; place 2 inches apart on greased baking sheets.

BAKE 8 minutes or just until set. (Do not overbake.) Let stand on baking sheet 1 minute; transfer to wire racks. Cool completely.

PLACE whipped topping and semi-sweet chocolate in microwaveable bowl. Microwave on HIGH 1½ minutes or until chocolate is completely melted and mixture is shiny and smooth, stirring after 1 minute. Let stand 15 minutes to thicken. Drizzle or spread over cookies. Let stand 40 minutes or until set.

Soft & Chewy Chocolate Drops

Chewy Apple Moons
Makes 1½ dozen cookies

¾ cup frozen unsweetened apple juice
   concentrate
½ cup coarsely chopped dried apples
2 eggs
¼ cup (½ stick) butter, melted and cooled
1 teaspoon vanilla

1¼ cups all-purpose flour
½ teaspoon baking powder
½ teaspoon ground cinnamon
¼ teaspoon salt
⅛ teaspoon ground nutmeg

1. Preheat oven to 350°F. Lightly grease or line cookie sheets with parchment paper.

2. Combine apple juice concentrate and apples in small bowl; let stand 10 minutes. Beat eggs in medium bowl. Beat in concentrate mixture, butter and vanilla. Add flour, baking powder, cinnamon, salt and nutmeg; mix well. Drop dough by tablespoonfuls 2 inches apart onto prepared cookie sheets.

3. Bake 12 minutes or until lightly browned. Cool on cookie sheets 2 minutes. Remove to wire racks; cool completely.

Moon Rocks
Makes 3 dozen cookies

1 package (18 ounces) refrigerated sugar
   cookie dough
1 cup quick oats

¾ cup butterscotch chips
¾ cup yogurt-covered raisins

1. Let dough stand at room temperature 15 minutes. Preheat oven to 350°F. Lightly grease or line cookie sheets with parchment paper.

2. Combine dough, oats, butterscotch chips and raisins in large bowl; beat with electric mixer at medium speed until well blended. Drop dough by rounded teaspoonfuls 2 inches apart onto prepared cookie sheets.

3. Bake 10 minutes or until set. Cool on cookie sheets 1 minute. Remove to wire racks; cool completely.

Chewy Apple Moons

Molasses Spice Cookies
Makes about 2½ dozen cookies

1¾ cups all-purpose flour
1 teaspoon baking soda
1 teaspoon ground ginger
1 teaspoon ground cinnamon
¼ teaspoon ground cloves
¼ teaspoon salt
1 cup granulated sugar

¾ cup (1½ sticks) butter or margarine, softened
1 large egg
¼ cup unsulphured molasses
2 cups (12-ounce package) NESTLÉ® TOLL HOUSE® Premier White Morsels
1 cup finely chopped walnuts

COMBINE flour, baking soda, ginger, cinnamon, cloves and salt in small bowl. Beat sugar and butter in large mixer bowl until creamy. Beat in egg and molasses. Gradually beat in flour mixture. Stir in morsels. Refrigerate for 20 minutes or until slightly firm.

PREHEAT oven to 375°F.

ROLL dough into 1-inch balls; roll in walnuts. Place on ungreased baking sheets.

BAKE for 9 to 11 minutes or until golden brown. Cool on baking sheets for 2 minutes; remove to wire racks to cool completely.

Prep Time: 40 minutes • **Bake Time:** 9 to 11 minutes

Molasses Spice Cookies

Berried Snowballs

Makes 2 dozen snowballs

¼ cup (½ stick) unsalted butter
4 cups mini marshmallows
4 cups crispy rice cereal

¾ to 1 cup sweetened dried cranberries
Vegetable oil
1½ cups flaked coconut

1. Melt butter in large heavy saucepan over low heat. Add marshmallows; cook and stir until melted. Remove from heat. (Or place butter and marshmallows in large microwavable bowl. Microwave on HIGH at 30-second intervals, stirring between each interval until melted and smooth.)

2. While mixture is still hot, add cereal and cranberries, stirring until well coated. With lightly oiled fingers, shape mixture into 24 (2-inch) balls. Roll balls in coconut. Let stand until cool.

Tip

Berried Snowballs can be frozen in resealable food storage bags or in airtight containers with waxed paper between the layers.

Berried Snowballs

Butterscotch Oatmeal Cookies

Makes about 3 dozen cookies

1¼ cups all-purpose flour
½ teaspoon salt
½ teaspoon baking soda
½ cup butterscotch chips
½ cup packed brown sugar
½ cup (1 stick) butter, softened
¼ cup granulated sugar

1 egg
1 teaspoon vanilla
¾ cup old-fashioned oats
½ cup shredded coconut
½ cup chopped pecans
Pecan halves (about 36)

1. Preheat oven to 350°F. Lightly grease or line cookie sheets with parchment paper.

2. Whisk flour, salt and baking soda in medium bowl. Place butterscotch chips in small microwavable bowl. Microwave on HIGH 1 minute; stir. Microwave at additional 30-second intervals until melted and smooth.

3. Beat brown sugar, butter and granulated sugar in large bowl with electric mixer at medium speed until light and fluffy. Add melted butterscotch chips, egg and vanilla; beat until well blended. Add flour mixture; beat just until blended. Stir in oats, coconut and chopped pecans.

4. Shape dough by level tablespoonfuls into balls; place 2 inches apart on prepared cookie sheets. Press 1 pecan half into center of each ball.

5. Bake 10 minutes or until edges are lightly browned. Cool on cookie sheets 1 minute. Remove to wire racks; cool completely.

Island Cookies
Makes about 3 dozen cookies

1⅔ cups all-purpose flour
¾ teaspoon baking powder
½ teaspoon baking soda
½ teaspoon salt
¾ cup (1½ sticks) butter, softened
¾ cup packed brown sugar
⅓ cup granulated sugar

1 teaspoon vanilla extract
1 large egg
1¾ cups (11.5-ounce package) NESTLÉ® TOLL HOUSE® Milk Chocolate Morsels
1 cup flaked coconut, toasted, if desired
1 cup chopped walnuts

PREHEAT oven to 375°F.

COMBINE flour, baking powder, baking soda and salt in small bowl. Beat butter, brown sugar, granulated sugar and vanilla extract in large mixer bowl until creamy. Beat in egg. Gradually beat in flour mixture. Stir in morsels, coconut and nuts. Drop by slightly rounded tablespoonful onto ungreased baking sheets.

BAKE for 8 to 11 minutes or until edges are lightly browned. Cool on baking sheets for 2 minutes; remove to wire racks to cool completely.

Note: NESTLÉ® TOLL HOUSE® Semi-Sweet Chocolate Morsels, Semi-Sweet Chocolate Mini Morsels, Premier White Morsels or Butterscotch Flavored Morsels can be substituted for the Milk Chocolate Morsels.

Island Cookies

Top-Notch Treats

Macadamia Nut White Chip Pumpkin Cookies
Makes about 4 dozen cookies

2 cups all-purpose flour
2 teaspoons ground cinnamon
1 teaspoon ground cloves
1 teaspoon baking soda
1 cup (2 sticks) butter or margarine, softened
½ cup granulated sugar
½ cup packed brown sugar

1 cup LIBBY'S® 100% Pure Pumpkin
1 large egg
2 teaspoons vanilla extract
2 cups (12-ounce package) NESTLÉ® TOLL HOUSE® Premier White Morsels
⅔ cup coarsely chopped macadamia nuts or walnuts, toasted

PREHEAT oven to 350°F.

COMBINE flour, cinnamon, cloves and baking soda in small bowl. Beat butter, granulated sugar and brown sugar in large mixer bowl until creamy. Beat in pumpkin, egg and vanilla extract until blended. Gradually beat in flour mixture. Stir in morsels and nuts. Drop by rounded tablespoonful onto greased baking sheets; flatten slightly with back of spoon or greased bottom of glass dipped in granulated sugar.

BAKE for 11 to 14 minutes or until centers are set. Cool on baking sheets for 2 minutes; remove to wire racks to cool completely.

Prep Time: 20 minutes • **Bake Time:** 11 to 14 minutes

Brandy Snaps with Lemon Ricotta Cream

Makes 2 dozen cookies

¾ cup sugar, divided
1 cup (2 sticks) butter, softened, divided
⅓ cup light corn syrup
1 cup all-purpose flour

1 tablespoon brandy or cognac
½ cup ricotta cheese
1 tablespoon lemon juice
2 teaspoons grated lemon peel

1. Preheat oven to 325°F.

2. Combine ½ cup sugar, ½ cup butter and corn syrup in medium saucepan; cook and stir over medium heat until butter is melted. Stir in flour and brandy. Drop batter by level tablespoonfuls about 3 inches apart onto ungreased cookie sheets, spacing to fit 4 cookies per sheet.

3. Bake, one cookie sheet at a time, 12 minutes or until lightly browned. Cool on cookie sheets 1 minute. Remove each cookie and quickly wrap around handle of wooden spoon.

4. Combine remaining ½ cup butter, ¼ cup sugar, ricotta, lemon juice and lemon peel in food processor or blender; process until smooth. Place filling in pastry bag fitted with plain or star tip. Fill cookies just before serving.

Tip

Unsalted butter has a more delicate flavor and is preferred by many cooks, especially for baking. Although it varies by manufacturer, salted butter has about 1½ teaspoons added salt per pound. Do not substitute whipped butter for regular butter in baked goods.

Brandy Snaps with Lemon Ricotta Cream

Chocolate Peppermint Macaroons

Makes 2 dozen macaroons

½ cup (4 ounces) chopped bittersweet
  chocolate
2 squares (1 ounce each) unsweetened
  chocolate
2 egg whites

⅛ teaspoon salt
½ cup sugar
½ teaspoon peppermint extract
2¾ cups flaked coconut
½ cup finely crushed peppermint candies*

About 18 peppermint candies will yield ½ cup finely crushed peppermints. To crush, place unwrapped candy in a heavy-duty resealable food storage bag. Loosely seal the bag, leaving an opening for air to escape. Crush with a rolling pin, meat mallet or the bottom of a heavy skillet.

1. Place bittersweet and unsweetened chocolate in medium microwavable bowl. Microwave on HIGH at 30-second intervals, stirring between each interval until melted and smooth. Let stand 15 minutes.

2. Preheat oven to 325°F. Lightly grease or line cookie sheets with parchment paper.

3. Beat egg whites and salt in large bowl with electric mixer at high speed until soft peaks form. Gradually add sugar; beat 5 minutes or until stiff peaks form. Add chocolate; beat at low speed just until blended. Stir in peppermint extract, scraping down sides of bowl. Fold in coconut.

4. Shape dough by level tablespoonfuls into 1-inch balls; place 2 inches apart on prepared cookie sheets. Make small indentation in center. Sprinkle crushed candy into indentations.

5. Bake 12 minutes or until outside is crisp and inside is moist and chewy. Cool on cookie sheets 2 minutes. Remove to wire racks; cool completely.

Chocolate Peppermint Macaroons

Chocolate Almond Sandwiches

Makes about 2½ dozen sandwich cookies

1 package (18 ounces) refrigerated sugar
  cookie dough
4 ounces almond paste
¼ cup all-purpose flour

1 container (16 ounces) dark chocolate
  frosting
Sliced almonds

1. Let dough stand at room temperature 15 minutes.

2. Beat dough, almond paste and flour in large bowl with electric mixer at medium speed until well blended. Divide dough into 3 pieces; freeze 20 minutes. Shape each piece into 10×1-inch log; wrap and refrigerate 2 hours or overnight. (Or freeze 1 hour or until firm.)

3. Preheat oven to 350°F. Lightly grease or line cookie sheets with parchment paper. Cut dough into ¼-inch slices; place 2 inches apart on prepared cookie sheets.

4. Bake 10 minutes or until edges are lightly browned. Cool on cookie sheets 2 minutes. Remove to wire racks; cool completely.

5. Spread frosting on flat sides of half of cookies; top with remaining cookies. Spread small amount of frosting on top of each sandwich cookie; top with 1 sliced almond.

Tip

Almond paste is a prepared product made of ground blanched almonds, sugar and an ingredient, such as glucose, glycerin or corn syrup, to keep it pliable. It is often used as an ingredient in confections and baked goods. Almond paste is available in cans and plastic tubes in most supermarkets or gourmet food markets. After opening, wrap the container tightly and store it in the refrigerator.

Chocolate Almond Sandwiches

Decadent Coconut Macaroons
Makes about 3 dozen cookies

1 package (14 ounces) flaked coconut
¾ cup sugar
6 tablespoons all-purpose flour
¼ teaspoon salt

4 egg whites
1 teaspoon vanilla
1 cup (6 ounces) semisweet or bittersweet
    chocolate chips, melted

1. Preheat oven to 325°F. Lightly grease and flour or line cookie sheets with parchment paper.

2. Combine coconut, sugar, flour and salt in large bowl. Beat in egg whites and vanilla with electric mixer at medium speed until blended. Drop batter by tablespoonfuls 2 inches apart onto prepared cookie sheets.

3. Bake 20 minutes or until set and edges are lightly browned. Remove to wire racks; cool completely. Dip cookies in melted chocolate; let stand until set.

KISSES® Cocoa Cookies
Makes about 4½ dozen cookies

1 cup (2 sticks) butter or margarine,
    softened
⅔ cup granulated sugar
1 teaspoon vanilla extract
1⅔ cups all-purpose flour

¼ cup HERSHEY'S Cocoa
1 cup finely chopped pecans
    About 54 HERSHEY'S KISSES® Brand
    Milk Chocolates
Powdered sugar

1. Beat butter, granulated sugar and vanilla in large bowl until creamy. Stir together flour and cocoa; gradually add to butter mixture, beating until well blended. Add pecans; beat until well blended. Refrigerate dough about 1 hour or until firm enough to handle.

2. Heat oven to 375°F. Remove wrappers from chocolate pieces. Mold scant tablespoon of dough around each chocolate piece, covering completely. Shape into balls. Place on ungreased cookie sheet.

3. Bake 10 to 12 minutes or until set. Cool about 1 minute; remove from cookie sheet to wire rack. Cool completely. Roll in powdered sugar. Roll in powdered sugar again just before serving, if desired.

Decadent Coconut Macaroons

Chocolate-Raspberry Kolacky

Makes about 1½ dozen cookies

2 squares (1 ounce each) semisweet
    chocolate, coarsely chopped
1½ cups all-purpose flour
¼ teaspoon baking soda
¼ teaspoon salt
½ cup (1 stick) butter, softened

1 package (3 ounces) cream cheese,
    softened
⅓ cup granulated sugar
1 teaspoon vanilla
    Seedless raspberry jam
    Powdered sugar

1. Place chocolate in small microwavable bowl. Microwave on HIGH 1 to 1½ minutes or until chocolate is melted, stirring after 1 minute. Cool slightly.

2. Whisk flour, baking soda and salt in small bowl. Beat butter and cream cheese in large bowl with electric mixer at medium speed until well blended. Beat in granulated sugar until light and fluffy. Beat in vanilla and melted chocolate until blended. Gradually add flour mixture, beating at low speed just until blended. Divide dough in half; shape each half into disc. Wrap and refrigerate 2 hours or until firm.

3. Preheat oven to 375°F. Lightly grease or line cookie sheets with parchment paper.

4. Working with one disc at a time, roll out dough between sheets of parchment paper to ¼- to ⅛-inch thickness. Cut out shapes with 3-inch round cookie cutter. Place 2 inches apart on prepared cookie sheets.

5. Place rounded ½ teaspoon jam in center of each circle. Bring three edges of dough circles up over jam; pinch edges together to seal, leaving center of triangle slightly open.

6. Bake 10 minutes or until set. Cool on cookie sheets 2 minutes. Remove to wire racks; cool completely.

7. Just before serving, sprinkle with powdered sugar. Store tightly covered in refrigerator; let stand 30 minutes at room temperature before serving.

Note: These cookies do not freeze well.

Chocolate-Raspberry Kolacky Cups: Grease 18 mini (1¾-inch) muffin cups. Fit dough circles into prepared muffin cups; fill with heaping teaspoonful jam. Bake 10 minutes or until set. Cool completely in pans on wire racks. Dust with powdered sugar before serving.

Chocolate-Raspberry Kolacky

Date Pinwheel Cookies

Makes 6 dozen cookies

3 cups plus 1 tablespoon all-purpose flour, divided

1¼ cups dates, pitted and finely chopped

¾ cup orange juice

½ cup granulated sugar

1 tablespoon butter

2 teaspoons vanilla, divided

1 cup packed brown sugar

½ (8-ounce) package cream cheese, softened

¼ cup (¼ stick) shortening

2 eggs

1 teaspoon baking soda

½ teaspoon salt

1. Heat 1 tablespoon flour, dates, orange juice, granulated sugar and butter in medium saucepan over medium heat. Cook 10 minutes or until thickened, stirring frequently. Remove from heat. Stir in 1 teaspoon vanilla; cool completely.

2. Beat brown sugar, cream cheese and shortening in large bowl with electric mixer at medium speed until light and fluffy. Add eggs and remaining 1 teaspoon vanilla; beat 2 minutes.

3. Whisk remaining 3 cups flour, baking soda and salt in medium bowl. Add to shortening mixture; stir just until blended. Divide dough in half. Roll out half of dough between sheets of parchment paper to 12×9-inch rectangle. Spread half of date mixture evenly over dough, leaving ¼-inch border at top short edge. Starting at opposite end, tightly roll up dough jelly-roll style. Wrap and freeze 1 hour. Repeat with remaining dough and date mixture.

4. Preheat oven to 350°F. Lightly grease or line cookie sheets with parchment paper. Using heavy thread or unflavored dental floss, cut dough into ¼-inch slices. Place 1 inch apart on prepared cookie sheets.

5. Bake 12 minutes or until lightly browned. Cool on cookie sheets 2 minutes. Remove to wire racks; cool completely.

Elephant Ears
Makes about 4 dozen cookies

1 package (17¼ ounces) frozen puff pastry, thawed according to package directions

1 egg, beaten

¼ cup sugar, divided

2 squares (1 ounce each) semisweet chocolate

1. Preheat oven to 375°F. Grease cookie sheets; sprinkle lightly with water.

2. Roll one sheet of pastry to 12×10-inch rectangle. Brush with egg; sprinkle with 1 tablespoon sugar. Tightly roll up 10-inch sides, meeting in center. Brush center with egg and seal rolls tightly together; turn over. Cut into ¼-inch-thick slices. Place slices 2 inches apart on prepared cookie sheets. Sprinkle with 1 tablespoon sugar. Repeat with remaining pastry, egg and sugar.

3. Bake 15 minutes or until lightly browned. Remove to wire racks; cool completely.

4. Melt chocolate in small heavy saucepan over low heat, stirring constantly. Spread bottoms of cookies with chocolate. Place chocolate side up on wire rack; let stand until set.

Berry Chocolate Cookie Tartlets
Makes 2 dozen tartlets

1¼ cups (about ⅓ tub) NESTLÉ® TOLL HOUSE® Refrigerated Sugar Cookie Tub Dough, slightly softened

⅓ cup plus 1 tablespoon all-purpose flour

½ cup NESTLÉ® TOLL HOUSE® Semi-Sweet Chocolate Morsels

½ cup dried cranberries or cherries, chopped

PREHEAT oven to 325°F.

COMBINE cookie dough and flour in large mixing bowl. Divide dough into 24 (1-inch) balls. Press dough into mini-muffin cups.*

BAKE for 10 minutes or until light golden brown around edges and puffy.

REMOVE tartlets from oven and immediately fill with morsels and cranberries. Cool for 10 minutes in muffin cups. Carefully remove to wire rack, do not invert; cool completely.

If making tartlets in batches, keep extra dough in the refrigerator.

Tip: Dough can be made in advance and refrigerated.

Elephant Ears

Espresso Cookie Cups
Makes 2 dozen cups

¼ cup (½ stick) unsalted butter
1 square (1 ounce) unsweetened chocolate, chopped
⅓ cup granulated sugar
2 tablespoons instant espresso powder
1 egg

1 teaspoon vanilla
2 tablespoons cake flour
¼ teaspoon salt
1 package (12 ounces) flaky honey-butter-flavored layered biscuits
Powdered sugar

1. Melt butter and chocolate in small heavy saucepan over low heat. Remove from heat; stir in granulated sugar and espresso powder. Whisk in egg and vanilla until blended. Stir in flour and salt.

2. Preheat oven to 350°F. Spray 24 mini (1¾-inch) muffin cups with nonstick cooking spray.

3. Separate individual biscuits, then pull each biscuit apart horizontally into 3 pieces each. Press each piece into bottom and up sides of muffin cups. Freeze 10 minutes.

4. Bake 6 minutes or until edges are lightly browned. While still warm, press bottom and sides of biscuits against pan with handle of wooden spoon to make well in center of cups. Fill centers with chocolate mixture.

5. Bake 7 minutes or until set. Remove to wire racks; cool completely. Dust with powdered sugar just before serving.

Tip
To easily dust cookies with powdered sugar, place a sheet of wax paper under the wire racks. Place powdered sugar in a small strainer and gently shake strainer over cooled cookies.

Espresso Cookie Cups

Linzer Sandwich Cookies
Makes about 2 dozen sandwich cookies

1⅔ cups all-purpose flour
¼ teaspoon baking powder
¼ teaspoon salt
¾ cup granulated sugar
½ cup (1 stick) butter, softened

1 egg
1 teaspoon vanilla
Seedless red raspberry jam
Powdered sugar

1. Whisk flour, baking powder and salt in small bowl. Beat granulated sugar and butter in medium bowl with electric mixer at medium speed until light and fluffy. Beat in egg and vanilla. Gradually add flour mixture, beating at low speed until dough forms. Divide dough in half; shape each half into disc. Wrap and refrigerate 2 hours or until firm.

2. Preheat oven to 375°F. Working with one disc at a time, roll out dough between sheets of parchment paper to ¼-inch thickness. Cut out shapes with fluted round cookie cutters. Cut out 1-inch centers from half of shapes. Place 1½ to 2 inches apart on ungreased cookie sheets. Repeat with trimmings.

3. Bake 8 minutes or until edges are lightly browned. Cool on cookie sheets 2 minutes. Remove to wire racks; cool completely.

4. Spread jam on flat sides of whole cookies, spreading almost to edges. Place cookies with cutouts over jam. Sprinkle cookies with powdered sugar.

Linzer Sandwich Cookies

Pebbernodders
Makes about 16 dozen cookies

3 cups all-purpose flour
1 teaspoon baking powder
1 teaspoon ground cinnamon
½ teaspoon ground ginger
½ teaspoon ground cloves

1½ cups sugar
1½ cups (3 sticks) butter, softened
3 eggs
2 teaspoons grated lemon peel

1. Whisk flour, baking powder, cinnamon, ginger and cloves in medium bowl. Beat sugar and butter in large bowl with electric mixer at medium speed until light and fluffy. Add eggs and lemon peel; beat until well blended. Gradually add flour mixture, beating just until blended.

2. Divide dough into four equal pieces; shape each piece into ¾-inch-thick rope about 12 inches long. Place ropes on prepared cookie sheets. Freeze 30 minutes or until firm.

3. Preheat oven to 375°F. Lightly grease or line cookie sheets with parchment paper. Cut ropes into ¼-inch-thick slices; place 1 inch apart on prepared cookie sheets.

4. Bake 10 minutes or until lightly browned. Cool on cookie sheets 2 minutes. Remove to wire racks; cool completely.

Pebbernodders

Swedish Sandwich Cookies (Syltkakor)

Makes 1½ dozen sandwich cookies

1 cup (2 sticks) unsalted butter, softened
½ cup plus 2 tablespoons sugar, divided
2 egg yolks
2 to 2¼ cups all-purpose flour

3 tablespoons ground almonds
1 egg white
⅔ cup strawberry or red currant jelly

1. Beat butter and ½ cup sugar in large bowl with electric mixer at medium speed until light and fluffy. Beat in egg yolks until well blended. Gradually add 1½ cups flour, beating at low speed until blended. Stir in additional flour to form stiff dough. Divide dough in half; shape each half into disc. Wrap and refrigerate 2 hours or until firm.

2. Preheat oven to 375°F. Lightly grease and flour or line cookie sheets with parchment paper.

3. Roll out one disc of dough between sheets of parchment paper to ¼-inch thickness. Cut out shapes with 2¼-inch round cookie cutter. Place 1½ to 2 inches apart on prepared cookie sheets. Gently knead dough trimmings; reroll and cut out additional shapes.

4. Roll out remaining disc of dough between sheets of parchment paper to ¼-inch thickness. Cut out shapes with 2¼-inch fluted cookie cutter. Cut out 1-inch centers. Place 1½ to 2 inches apart on prepared cookie sheets. (Cut equal numbers of round and scalloped cookies.)

5. Combine almonds and remaining 2 tablespoons sugar in small bowl. Brush each fluted cookie with egg white; sprinkle with sugar mixture.

6. Bake 8 minutes or until set and lightly browned. Cool on cookie sheets 2 minutes. Remove cookies to wire racks; cool completely.

7. Spread jelly over flat sides of round cookies; top with fluted cookies.

Rosemary Honey Shortbread Cookies

Makes 2 dozen cookies

2 cups all-purpose flour
1 tablespoon fresh rosemary leaves,*
    minced
½ teaspoon salt

½ teaspoon baking powder
¾ cup (1½ sticks) unsalted butter, softened
½ cup powdered sugar
2 tablespoons honey

For best flavor, use only fresh rosemary or substitute fresh or dried lavender buds.

1. Whisk flour, rosemary, salt and baking powder in medium bowl. Beat butter, powdered sugar and honey in large bowl with electric mixer at medium speed until light and fluffy. Beat in flour mixture just until blended. (Mixture will be crumbly.)

2. Shape dough into 12-inch log. Wrap and refrigerate 1 hour or until firm. (Dough can be refrigerated several days before baking.)

3. Preheat oven to 350°F. Lightly grease or line cookie sheets with parchment paper. Shape dough into 12-inch log. Cut log into ½-inch slices. Place 2 inches apart on prepared cookie sheets.

4. Bake 13 minutes or until set. Cool on cookie sheets 1 minute. Remove to wire racks; cool completely.

Rosemary Honey Shortbread Cookies

Pumpkin Whoopie Minis
Makes about 2½ dozen sandwich cookies

1¾ cups all-purpose flour
2 teaspoons pumpkin pie spice
1 teaspoon baking powder
1 teaspoon baking soda
1 teaspoon salt, divided
1 cup packed brown sugar
½ cup (1 stick) butter, softened, divided

1 cup solid-pack pumpkin
2 eggs, lightly beaten
¼ cup vegetable oil
1 teaspoon vanilla, divided
4 ounces cream cheese, softened
1½ cups powdered sugar

1. Preheat oven to 350°F. Lightly grease or line cookie sheets with parchment paper.

2. Whisk flour, pumpkin pie spice, baking powder, baking soda and ¾ teaspoon salt in medium bowl. Beat brown sugar and ¼ cup butter in large bowl with electric mixer at medium speed until light and fluffy. Beat in pumpkin, eggs, oil and ½ teaspoon vanilla until well blended. Beat in flour at low speed just until blended. Drop dough by teaspoonfuls 2 inches apart onto prepared cookie sheets.

3. Bake 10 minutes or until set. Cool on cookie sheets 5 minutes. Remove to wire racks; cool completely.

4. Meanwhile, prepare filling. Beat cream cheese and remaining ¼ cup butter in medium bowl with electric mixer at medium speed until creamy. Beat in remaining ½ teaspoon vanilla and ¼ teaspoon salt until blended. Gradually add powdered sugar, beating well after each addition.

5. Spoon filling onto flat sides of half of cookies; top with remaining cookies. Store in airtight container in refrigerator.

Pumpkin Whoopie Minis

Chocolate Hazelnut Biscottini

Makes about 4½ dozen biscottini

2½ cups all-purpose flour

1 teaspoon baking powder

½ teaspoon salt

½ teaspoon ground cinnamon

¾ cup (1½ sticks) unsalted butter, softened

⅓ cup chocolate-hazelnut spread

¾ cup sugar

2 eggs

1 cup coarsely chopped toasted hazelnuts*

1 cup milk chocolate chips

*To toast hazelnuts, spread in single layer in medium skillet. Cook over medium heat 2 minutes, stirring frequently, or until skins begin to peel and nuts are lightly browned. Transfer to clean dish towel; rub hazelnuts to remove skins. Cool completely.

1. Whisk flour, baking powder, salt and cinnamon in medium bowl. Beat butter and chocolate-hazelnut spread in large bowl with electric mixer at medium speed until light and fluffy. Add sugar; beat until blended. Add eggs, one at a time, beating well after each addition. Add flour mixture, ½ cup at a time, beating well after each addition. Add hazelnuts and chocolate chips; stir just until blended.

2. Shape dough into two 13×2-inch logs on prepared baking sheet; gently pat to smooth top. Refrigerate 3 to 4 hours.

3. Preheat oven to 350°F. Lightly grease cookie sheet or line with parchment paper.

4. Bake 25 minutes or until set and lightly browned. Remove from oven. Cool on baking sheet 10 minutes.

5. *Reduce oven temperature to 325°F.* With serrated knife, cut each log into 1-inch-thick slices; cut each slice in half. Arrange slices on baking sheet.

6. Bake 15 minutes. Cool on baking sheet 5 minutes. Turn slices; bake 15 minutes. Cool completely on baking sheet on wire rack.

Chocolate Hazelnut Biscottini

Chocolate Decadence

Deep Dark Chocolate Drops
Makes about 3 dozen cookies

1½ cups semisweet chocolate chips, divided

1¼ cups all-purpose flour

¼ cup unsweetened cocoa powder

½ teaspoon salt

½ teaspoon baking soda

½ cup granulated sugar

½ cup (1 stick) butter, softened

¼ cup packed brown sugar

1 egg

2 tablespoons milk

1 teaspoon vanilla

1. Preheat oven to 350°F. Lightly grease or line cookie sheets with parchment paper.

2. Place ½ cup chocolate chips in small microwavable bowl. Microwave on HIGH 1 minute; stir. Microwave at additional 30-second intervals, stirring after each interval until melted and smooth. Cool slightly.

3. Whisk flour, cocoa, salt and baking soda in medium bowl. Beat granulated sugar, butter and brown sugar in large bowl with electric mixer at medium speed until light and fluffy. Add egg, milk, vanilla and melted chocolate; beat until well blended. Add flour mixture; beat just until blended. Stir in remaining 1 cup chocolate chips.

4. Drop dough by rounded tablespoonfuls 2 inches apart onto prepared cookie sheets.

5. Bake 10 minutes or until set. Cool on cookie sheets 2 minutes. Remove to wire racks; cool completely.

Chocolate Pistachio Cookies

Makes about 3½ dozen cookies

2 cups shelled pistachio or macadamia nuts, finely chopped

1¾ cups all-purpose flour

¼ cup unsweetened cocoa powder

¾ teaspoon baking soda

½ teaspoon salt

¾ cup plus 1 tablespoon I CAN'T BELIEVE IT'S NOT BUTTER!® Spread

1 cup granulated sugar

¾ cup firmly packed brown sugar

2 eggs

3 squares (1 ounce each) unsweetened chocolate, melted

½ teaspoon vanilla extract

⅛ teaspoon almond extract

1½ squares (1 ounce each) unsweetened chocolate

2 tablespoons confectioners' sugar

Preheat oven to 375°F. Lightly spray baking sheets with I Can't Believe It's Not Butter!® Spray; set aside. Reserve 3 tablespoons pistachios for garnish.

In medium bowl, combine flour, cocoa powder, baking soda and salt; set aside.

In large bowl with electric mixer, beat ¾ cup I Can't Believe It's Not Butter!® Spread, granulated sugar and brown sugar until light and fluffy, about 5 minutes. Beat in eggs, one at a time, beating 30 seconds after each addition. Beat in melted chocolate and extracts. Beat in flour mixture just until blended. Stir in pistachios.

On prepared baking sheets, drop dough by rounded tablespoonfuls 1 inch apart. Bake, one sheet at a time, 8 minutes or until tops are puffed and dry but still soft when touched. Do not overbake. On wire rack, cool 5 minutes; remove from sheets and cool completely.

For icing, in microwave-safe bowl, melt 1½ squares chocolate with remaining 1 tablespoon I Can't Believe It's Not Butter! Spread at HIGH (100%) 1 minute or until chocolate is melted; stir until smooth. Stir in confectioners' sugar. Lightly spread ¼ teaspoon icing on each cookie, then sprinkle with reserved pistachios. Let stand 20 minutes before serving.

Chocolate Pistachio Cookies

Cocoa Crackles

Makes about 3½ dozen cookies

1½ cups all-purpose flour
⅓ cup unsweetened cocoa powder
½ teaspoon salt
½ teaspoon baking soda
½ cup granulated sugar

½ cup (1 stick) butter, softened
¼ cup packed light brown sugar
2 eggs
1 teaspoon vanilla
Powdered sugar

1. Preheat oven to 350°F. Lightly grease or line cookie sheets with parchment paper.

2. Combine flour, cocoa, salt and baking soda in medium bowl. Beat granulated sugar, butter and brown sugar in large bowl with electric mixer at medium speed until light and fluffy. Add eggs and vanilla; beat until well blended. Add flour mixture; beat just until blended.

3. Place powdered sugar in shallow bowl. Shape heaping teaspoonfuls of dough into balls. Roll in powdered sugar; place 2 inches apart on prepared cookie sheets.

4. Bake 11 minutes or until set and no longer shiny. Cool on cookie sheets 2 minutes. Remove to wire racks; cool completely.

Tip

Electric mixers come in many styles and sizes. Portable hand-held and stand mixers are available. Portable mixers can do most of the operations of stand mixers, but they sometimes have difficulty with heavy doughs. (They also leave you with only one free hand.) The frequent baker may find the stand mixer more practical. Select one with a dough hook and whip for more versatility. If you choose to have only a portable mixer, buy a high quality one that is comfortable to hold.

Cocoa Crackles

Decadent Cocoa-Oatmeal Cookies

Makes 4 dozen cookies

½ cup (1 stick) unsalted butter, softened
½ cup granulated sugar
½ cup packed brown sugar
1 egg
½ teaspoon vanilla
¾ cup all-purpose flour

¼ cup unsweetened cocoa powder
½ teaspoon baking powder
1½ cups quick oats
1 cup milk chocolate chips
½ cup chopped macadamia nuts, toasted*

*To toast macadamia nuts, preheat oven to 350°F. Spread nuts on ungreased baking sheet. Bake 5 to 7 minutes, stirring occasionally, or until brown.

1. Preheat oven to 350°F. Lightly grease or line cookie sheets with parchment paper.

2. Beat butter in medium bowl with electric mixer at medium speed until light and fluffy. Add granulated sugar and brown sugar; beat until well blended. Add egg and vanilla; beat just until combined. Add flour, cocoa and baking powder; beat at low speed just until blended. (Dough will be sticky.) Stir in oats, chocolate chips and nuts.

3. Shape tablespoonfuls of dough into 1-inch balls. Place 2 inches apart on prepared cookie sheets. Slightly flatten each ball with back of spoon.

4. Bake 8 minutes or until set. Cool on cookie sheets 5 minutes. Remove to wire racks; cool completely.

Chocolate Pinwheels
Makes about 3½ dozen cookies

2 cups (4 sticks) unsalted butter, softened
1 cup powdered sugar
¼ cup packed light brown sugar
½ teaspoon salt

4 cups all-purpose flour
½ cup semisweet chocolate chips, melted
1 tablespoon unsweetened cocoa

1. Beat butter, powdered sugar, brown sugar and salt in large bowl with electric mixer at medium speed 2 minutes or until light and fluffy. Gradually add flour, beating until well blended.

2. Divide dough in half; set one half aside. Add melted chocolate and cocoa to remaining dough; beat until well blended.

3. Shape chocolate and plain doughs into 4 balls each. Roll out 1 ball plain dough between sheets of parchment paper to 12×6-inch rectangle. Roll out 1 ball chocolate dough between sheets of parchment paper to 12×6-inch rectangle; place over plain dough. Starting at wide end, tightly roll up jelly-roll style to form 12-inch log. If dough crumbles or breaks, press back together and continue to roll (the effect will be marbled, not spiralled, but just as attractive). Wrap and refrigerate 1 hour. Repeat with remaining dough.

4. Preheat oven to 300°F. Cut each log into 20 slices; place 2 inches apart on ungreased cookie sheets.

5. Bake 13 minutes or until set and lightly browned. Cool on cookie sheets 5 minutes. Remove to wire racks; cool completely.

Chocolate Pinwheels

Mint Chocolate Delights

Makes 2 dozen sandwich cookies

1 cup (2 sticks) unsalted butter, softened, divided
½ cup granulated sugar
⅓ cup packed dark brown sugar
⅓ cup semisweet chocolate chips, melted and slightly cooled
1 egg
½ teaspoon vanilla

1½ cups all-purpose flour
¼ cup unsweetened cocoa powder
½ teaspoon salt, divided
2½ cups powdered sugar
½ teaspoon mint extract
3 to 4 drops red food coloring
2 to 3 tablespoons milk or half-and-half

1. Beat ½ cup butter, granulated sugar and brown sugar in large bowl with electric mixer at medium speed until light and fluffy. Add melted chocolate, egg and vanilla; beat until well blended.

2. Whisk flour, cocoa and ¼ teaspoon salt in small bowl. Gradually add to butter mixture, beating well after each addition. Shape dough into 16-inch log. Wrap and refrigerate 1 hour or until firm.

3. Preheat oven to 400°F. Lightly grease or line cookie sheets with parchment paper. Cut log into ¼-inch slices. Place 2 inches apart on prepared cookie sheets.

4. Bake 10 minutes or until set. Cool on cookie sheets 5 minutes. Remove to wire racks; cool completely.

5. Beat powdered sugar, remaining ½ cup butter and ¼ teaspoon salt in large bowl with electric mixer at medium speed until well blended. Add mint extract and food coloring; beat until well blended. Beat in milk, 1 tablespoon at a time, until light and fluffy. Spread filling on flat sides of half of cookies; top with remaining cookies.

Mocha Dots

Makes about 6½ dozen cookies

1 tablespoon instant coffee granules
2 tablespoons hot water
1½ cups all-purpose flour
¼ cup unsweetened cocoa powder
½ teaspoon salt
½ teaspoon baking soda
½ cup granulated sugar

½ cup (1 stick) butter, softened
¼ cup packed light brown sugar
1 egg
1 teaspoon vanilla
Chocolate nonpareil candies
  (about 1 inch in diameter)

1. Preheat oven to 350°F. Lightly grease or line cookie sheets with parchment paper.

2. Dissolve instant coffee granules in hot water in small bowl; cool slightly. Whisk flour, cocoa, salt and baking soda in medium bowl.

3. Beat granulated sugar, butter and brown sugar in large bowl with electric mixer at medium speed until light and fluffy. Add coffee mixture, egg and vanilla; beat until well blended. Add flour mixture; beat until well blended.

4. Shape dough by level teaspoonfuls into balls; place 2 inches apart on prepared cookie sheets. Gently press 1 candy onto center of each ball. (Do not press candies too far into dough balls. Cookies will spread around candies as they bake.)

5. Bake 8 minutes or until set and no longer shiny. Cool on cookie sheets 2 minutes. Remove to wire racks; cool completely.

Mocha Dots

Fudgey German Chocolate Sandwich Cookies

Makes about 1½ dozen sandwich cookies

1¾ cups all-purpose flour

1½ cups sugar

¾ cup (1½ sticks) butter or margarine,
   softened

⅔ cup HERSHEY₂S Cocoa or HERSHEY₂S
   SPECIAL DARK® Cocoa

¾ teaspoon baking soda

¼ teaspoon salt

2 eggs

2 tablespoons milk

1 teaspoon vanilla extract

½ cup finely chopped pecans

   Coconut and Pecan Filling (recipe follows)

1. Heat oven to 350°F.

2. Combine flour, sugar, butter, cocoa, baking soda, salt, eggs, milk and vanilla in large bowl. Beat at medium speed of mixer until blended (batter will be stiff). Stir in pecans.

3. Form dough into 1¼-inch balls. Place on ungreased cookie sheet; flatten slightly.

4. Bake 9 to 11 minutes or until almost set. Cool slightly; remove from cookie sheet to wire rack. Cool completely. Spread about 1 heaping tablespoon Coconut and Pecan Filling onto bottom of one cookie. Top with second cookie to make sandwich. Serve warm or at room temperature.

Coconut and Pecan Filling

Makes about 2 cups filling

½ cup (1 stick) butter or margarine

½ cup packed light brown sugar

¼ cup light corn syrup

1 cup MOUNDS® Sweetened Coconut
   Flakes, toasted*

1 cup finely chopped pecans

1 teaspoon vanilla extract

*To toast coconut, heat oven to 350°F. Spread coconut in even layer on baking sheet. Bake 6 to 8 minutes, stirring occasionally, until golden.

Melt butter in medium saucepan over medium heat; add brown sugar and corn syrup. Stir constantly until thick and bubbly. Remove from heat; stir in coconut, pecans and vanilla. Use warm.

Fudgey German Chocolate Sandwich Cookies

Dark Cocoa Spice Cookies

Makes about 5 dozen cookies

2½ cups all-purpose flour
½ cup unsweetened Dutch process cocoa powder
1 teaspoon ground cinnamon
1 teaspoon ground cardamom
½ teaspoon baking soda
¼ teaspoon salt
1½ cups packed dark brown sugar

1 cup (2 sticks) unsalted butter, softened
2 egg yolks
1 teaspoon coconut extract
1¼ cups sifted powdered sugar
1 egg white
Pinch cream of tartar
Decorating sugar or demerara sugar

1. Sift flour, cocoa, cinnamon, cardamom, baking soda and salt into medium bowl.

2. Beat brown sugar and butter in large bowl with electric mixer at medium speed until light and fluffy. Beat in egg yolks and coconut extract. Add flour mixture; beat until blended.

3. Gather dough into ball and divide into 4 equal pieces. Shape each piece into 6-inch log. Wrap and refrigerate 4 hours or overnight.

4. Preheat oven to 325°F. Lightly grease or line cookie sheets with parchment paper. Cut each log into 16 slices. Place 1 inch apart on prepared cookie sheets.

5. Bake 12 minutes or until set. Cool on cookie sheets 5 minutes. Remove to wire racks; cool completely.

6. Beat powdered sugar, egg white and cream of tartar in small bowl with electric mixer at medium speed until thick and smooth. Cover with damp cloth during use to prevent icing from drying out. Use small paintbrush to brush edges of cooled cookies with icing, then roll edges in sugar before icing hardens.

Shipping Tip: To help cookies survive during shipping, place them in cupcake liners and nestle them snugly into a gift box or tin.

Chocolate-Dipped Oat Cookies
Makes about 6 dozen cookies

2 cups old-fashioned oats
¾ cup packed brown sugar
½ cup finely chopped walnuts
½ cup vegetable oil

1 egg
2 teaspoons grated orange peel
¼ teaspoon salt
1 package (12 ounces) milk chocolate chips

1. Combine oats, brown sugar, walnuts, oil, egg, orange peel and salt in large bowl until blended. Cover and refrigerate overnight.

2. Preheat oven to 350°F. Lightly grease or line cookie sheets with parchment paper.

3. Melt chocolate chips in top of double boiler over simmering water; keep warm. Shape oat mixture into large marble-size balls. Place 2 inches apart on prepared cookie sheets.

4. Bake 10 minutes or until lightly browned and crisp. Cool on cookie sheets 1 minute. Remove to wire racks; cool 10 minutes.

5. Dip top of each cookie in melted chocolate. Place on waxed paper; let stand until set.

Tip
A double boiler consists of two stacked pans and a cover. The top pan, which holds food, nestles in the bottom pan, which holds simmering water. The purpose of a double boiler is to protect heat-sensitive foods from direct heat, making it the perfect choice for melting chocolate.

Chocolate-Dipped Oat Cookies

Chocolate Malt Delights

Makes about 1½ dozen cookies

1 package (18 ounces) refrigerated
    chocolate chip cookie dough
⅓ cup plus 3 tablespoons malted milk
    powder, divided

1¼ cups prepared chocolate frosting
1 cup coarsely chopped malted milk balls

1. Let dough stand at room temperature 15 minutes. Preheat oven to 350°F. Lightly grease or line cookie sheets with parchment paper.

2. Beat dough and ⅓ cup malted milk powder in large bowl with electric mixer at medium speed until well blended. Drop dough by rounded tablespoonfuls onto prepared cookie sheets.

3. Bake 10 minutes or until edges are lightly browned. Cool on cookie sheets 5 minutes. Remove to wire racks; cool completely.

4. Combine frosting and remaining 3 tablespoons malted milk powder. Top each cookie with rounded tablespoonful of frosting mixture; garnish with malted milk balls.

Pastel Mint Swirls

Makes about 4 dozen cookies

⅓ cup coarse or granulated sugar
1 package (about 18 ounces) devil's food
    cake mix without pudding in the mix
3 eggs

¼ cup unsweetened cocoa powder
¼ cup (½ stick) butter, melted
1½ cups small pastel mint chips

1. Preheat oven to 375°F. Place sugar in shallow bowl.

2. Combine cake mix, eggs, cocoa and butter in large bowl just until blended. (Dough will be stiff.)

3. Shape dough by tablespoonfuls into 1-inch balls; roll in sugar to coat. Place 2 inches apart on ungreased cookie sheets.

4. Bake 8 minutes or until tops are cracked. Gently press 3 mint chips into top of each cookie. Cool on cookie sheets 1 minute. Remove to wire racks; cool completely.

Chocolate Malt Delights

Oatmeal-Chip Crispies
Makes about 6 dozen cookies

2 cups all-purpose flour
1 teaspoon baking powder
1 teaspoon baking soda
½ teaspoon salt
1 cup (2 sticks) butter, softened
1 cup packed brown sugar
¾ cup granulated sugar

2 eggs
1 teaspoon grated orange peel
1 tablespoon orange juice
2 cup old-fashioned oats
1 cup dried cranberries
¾ cup white chocolate chips
¾ cup semisweet chocolate chips

1. Preheat oven to 350°F. Lightly grease or line cookie sheets with parchment paper.

2. Combine flour, baking powder, baking soda and salt in medium bowl. Beat butter, brown sugar and granulated sugar in large bowl with electric mixer at medium speed 2 minutes. Add eggs, orange peel and orange juice; beat 1 minute. Add flour mixture; beat until well blended. Stir in oats, cranberries and chocolate chips until well blended.

3. Shape dough into 1-inch balls. Place 1½ inches apart on prepared cookie sheets. Flatten slightly to ½-inch thickness.

4. Bake 15 to 17 minutes or until lightly brown and firm to the touch. Cool on cookie sheets 2 minutes. Remove to wire racks; cool completely.

Oatmeal-Chip Crispies

Double Chocolate Peanut Butter Thumbprint Cookies

Makes 3 dozen cookies

1½ cups all-purpose flour
⅓ cup NESTLÉ® TOLL HOUSE® Baking
    Cocoa
1½ teaspoons baking powder
¼ teaspoon salt
2 cups (12-ounce package) NESTLÉ® TOLL
    HOUSE® Semi-Sweet Chocolate
    Morsels, divided

1 cup granulated sugar
1 cup chunky or smooth peanut butter
    (not all-natural), divided
⅓ cup butter or margarine, softened
1½ teaspoons vanilla extract
2 large eggs

PREHEAT oven to 350°F.

COMBINE flour, cocoa, baking powder and salt in small bowl. Melt *1 cup* morsels in small *heavy-duty* saucepan over low heat; stir until smooth. Beat granulated sugar, *⅓ cup* peanut butter, butter and vanilla extract in large mixer bowl until creamy. Beat in melted chocolate. Add eggs, one at a time, beating well after each addition. Gradually beat in cocoa mixture. Stir in *remaining 1 cup* morsels. Cover; refrigerate just until firm.

SHAPE into 1½-inch balls. Place 2 inches apart on ungreased baking sheets. Press thumb into tops to make about ½-inch-deep depressions. Fill each depression with about *½ teaspoon* peanut butter.

BAKE for 10 to 15 minutes or until sides are set but centers are still slightly soft. Cool on baking sheets for 2 minutes; remove to wire racks to cool completely.

Prep Time: 45 minutes • **Bake Time:** 10 to 15 minutes • **Cool Time:** 2 minutes

Double Chocolate Peanut Butter Thumbprint Cookies

Chocolate-Frosted Marshmallow Cookies

Makes about 5 dozen cookies

¾ cup (1½ sticks) butter, divided

3½ squares (1 ounce each) unsweetened chocolate, divided

1 cup packed brown sugar

1 egg

1 teaspoon vanilla

½ teaspoon baking soda

1½ cups all-purpose flour

½ cup milk

1 package (16 ounces) marshmallows, halved crosswise

1½ cups powdered sugar

1 egg white

1 teaspoon vanilla

1. Preheat oven to 350°F. Lightly grease or line cookie sheets with parchment paper.

2. Melt ½ cup butter and 2 squares chocolate in small heavy saucepan over low heat, stirring until smooth. Remove from heat; cool slightly.

3. Beat brown sugar, egg, vanilla and baking soda in large bowl with electric mixer at medium speed until light and fluffy. Beat in chocolate mixture and flour until smooth. Beat in milk at low speed until blended. Drop dough by teaspoonfuls 2 inches apart onto prepared cookie sheets.

4. Bake 10 minutes or until set. Immediately place marshmallow half, cut side down, on each baked cookie. Bake 1 minute or just until marshmallow is warm enough to stick to cookie. Remove to wire racks; cool completely.

5. Melt remaining ¼ cup butter and 1½ squares chocolate in small heavy saucepan over low heat, stirring until smooth. Beat in powdered sugar until well blended. Beat in egg white and vanilla, adding a little water, if necessary, to make smooth, slightly soft frosting. Spoon frosting over cookies to cover marshmallows.

Chocolate-Frosted Marshmallow Cookies

Chocolate Sugar Cookies
Makes about 3½ dozen cookies

2 cups flour
1 teaspoon baking soda
¼ teaspoon salt
3 squares BAKER'S® Unsweetened Baking
    Chocolate

1 cup (2 sticks) butter or margarine
1 cup sugar
1 egg
1 teaspoon vanilla
    Additional sugar

HEAT oven to 375°F. Mix flour, baking soda and salt in medium bowl; set aside.

MICROWAVE chocolate and butter in large microwavable bowl on HIGH 2 minutes or until butter is melted. Stir until chocolate is completely melted.

STIR sugar into chocolate mixture until well blended. Mix in egg and vanilla. Stir in flour mixture until well blended. Refrigerate dough about 15 minutes or until easy to handle.

SHAPE dough into 1-inch balls; roll in additional sugar. Place on ungreased cookie sheets.

BAKE 8 to 10 minutes. (If a flatter, crisper cookie is desired, flatten with bottom of glass before baking.) Cool on cookie sheets 1 minute. Remove to wire racks and cool completely.

Jam-Filled Chocolate Sugar Cookies: Prepare dough as directed. Roll in finely chopped nuts in place of sugar. Make indentation in each ball; fill center with your favorite jam. Bake as directed.

Chocolate-Caramel Sugar Cookies: Prepare dough as directed. Roll in finely chopped nuts in place of sugar. Make indentation in each ball; bake as directed. Microwave 1 package (14 ounces) caramels and 2 tablespoons milk in microwavable bowl on HIGH 3 minutes or until melted, stirring after 2 minutes. Fill centers of cookies with caramel mixture. Drizzle with melted BAKER'S® Semi-Sweet Baking Chocolate.

Prep Time: 20 minutes • **Bake Time:** 8 to 10 minutes

Chocolate Sugar Cookies

Kiddie Creations

Monogram Cookies
Makes 2 dozen cookies

3½ cups all-purpose flour
1 teaspoon salt
1½ cups sugar
1 cup (2 sticks) unsalted butter, softened
2 eggs

2 teaspoons vanilla
Gel food coloring
1 container (16 ounces) white or vanilla frosting
Assorted jumbo nonpareils (optional)

1. Whisk flour and salt in medium bowl. Beat sugar and butter in large bowl with electric mixer at medium speed until light and fluffy. Add eggs, one at a time, beating well after each addition. Add vanilla; beat until blended.

2. Gradually add flour mixture, beating well after each addition. Divide dough in half; shape each half into disc. Wrap and refrigerate 1 hour.

3. Preheat oven to 350°F. Lightly grease or line cookie sheets with parchment paper.

4. Working with one disc at a time, roll out dough between sheets of parchment paper to ¼-inch thickness. Cut out circles with 3-inch fluted round cookie cutter. Place 1 inch apart on prepared cookie sheets. Cut out letters using 1-inch alphabet cookie cutters; discard. Refrigerate 15 minutes.

5. Bake 15 minutes or until set. Cool on cookie sheets 5 minutes. Remove to wire racks; cool completely.

6. Add food coloring, a few drops at a time, to frosting; stir until evenly tinted. Spread cookies with frosting. Decorate with nonpareils, if desired. Let stand 10 minutes or until set.

Cupcake Cookies
Makes 2 dozen cookies

3½ cups all-purpose flour
1 teaspoon salt
1½ cups sugar
1 cup (2 sticks) unsalted butter, softened
2 eggs

2 teaspoons vanilla
1½ containers (16 ounces each) white
or vanilla frosting
Assorted gel food colorings
Large confetti sprinkles

1. Whisk flour and salt in medium bowl. Beat sugar and butter in large bowl with electric mixer at medium speed until light and fluffy. Add eggs, one at a time, beating well after each addition. Add vanilla; beat until blended.

2. Gradually add flour mixture, beating well after each addition. Divide dough in half; shape each half into disc. Wrap and refrigerate 1 hour.

3. Preheat oven to 350°F. Lightly grease or line cookie sheets with parchment paper.

4. Working with one disc at a time, roll out dough between sheets of parchment paper to ¼-inch thickness. Cut out cupcake shapes with sharp knife (approximately 2½×2½-inch shapes). Place 1 inch apart on prepared cookie sheets. Refrigerate 15 minutes.

5. Bake 15 minutes or until set. Cool on cookie sheets 5 minutes. Remove to wire racks; cool completely.

6. Reserve half of frosting. Add food coloring, a few drops at a time, to remaining half of frosting; stir until evenly tinted. Spread bottom half of cookies with frosting. Let stand 3 minutes or until just beginning to set. Press toothpick into frosting to create lines that resemble muffin cups. Let stand on wire racks 10 minutes or until set.

7. Add food coloring, a few drops at a time, to reserved frosting; stir until evenly tinted. (Divide frosting before adding food coloring if more colors are desired.) Spread top halves of cookies with frosting. Press sprinkles into frosting. Let stand 10 minutes or until set.

Cupcake Cookies

Go Fly a Kite Cookies

Makes about 1½ dozen cookies

3½ cups all-purpose flour
1 teaspoon salt
1½ cups sugar
1 cup (2 sticks) unsalted butter, softened
2 eggs

2 teaspoons vanilla
Royal Icing (recipe follows)
Blue and green gel food colorings
Yellow decorating icing

1. Whisk flour and salt in medium bowl. Beat sugar and butter in large bowl with electric mixer at medium speed until light and fluffy. Add eggs, one at a time, beating well after each addition. Add vanilla; beat until blended.

2. Gradually add flour mixture, beating well after each addition. Divide dough in half; shape each half into disc. Wrap and refrigerate 1 hour.

3. Preheat oven to 350°F. Lightly grease or line cookie sheets with parchment paper.

4. Working with one disc at a time, roll out dough between sheets of parchment paper to ¼-inch thickness. Cut out circles with 3¼-inch round cookie cutter. Place 1 inch apart on prepared cookie sheets. Refrigerate 15 minutes.

5. Bake 15 minutes or until set. Cool on cookie sheets 5 minutes. Remove to wire racks; cool completely.

6. Prepare Royal Icing. Reserve ¾ cup Royal Icing in medium bowl. Add blue food coloring, a few drops at a time, to remaining icing to create sky blue; stir until evenly tinted. Spread cookies with sky blue icing. Let stand 10 minutes or until set.

7. Pipe clouds using ¼ cup reserved white icing. Divide remaining ½ cup white icing into 2 small bowls. Add food coloring, a few drops at a time, to each bowl to make dark blue and green icings; stir until evenly tinted. Pipe kites using dark blue and green icings. Pipe kite tails using yellow decorating icing. Let stand 10 minutes or until set.

Royal Icing: Combine 4 cups powdered sugar, ¼ cup plus 2 tablespoons water and 3 tablespoons meringue powder in medium bowl. Beat with electric mixer at high speed 7 minutes or until soft peaks form. Cover surface with plastic wrap until needed. Makes about 2 cups.

Go Fly a Kite Cookies

Mischievous Monkeys

Makes 10 cookies

3 cups all-purpose flour
½ cup unsweetened cocoa powder
1 teaspoon salt
1½ cups sugar
1 cup (2 sticks) unsalted butter, softened
2 eggs

1 teaspoon vanilla
Yellow gel food coloring
1 cup prepared white or vanilla frosting
Black string licorice
20 brown candy-coated peanut butter candies

1. Whisk flour, cocoa and salt in medium bowl. Beat sugar and butter in large bowl with electric mixer at medium speed until light and fluffy. Add eggs, one at a time, beating well after each addition. Add vanilla; beat until blended.

2. Gradually add flour mixture, beating well after each addition. Divide dough in half; shape each half into disc. Wrap and refrigerate 1 hour.

3. Preheat oven to 350°F. Lightly grease or line cookie sheets with parchment paper.

4. Working with one disc at a time, roll out dough between sheets of parchment paper to ¼-inch thickness. From each disc, cut out 5 large circles with 3-inch round cookie cutter, 5 medium circles with 2-inch round cookie cutter and 10 small circles with 1½-inch round cookie cutter.

5. Place large circles 3 inches apart on prepared cookie sheets. Place 2 small circles next to each large circle for ears. Place medium circles 1 inch apart on separate prepared cookie sheet. Refrigerate 15 minutes.

6. Bake circles 12 minutes or until set. Cool on cookie sheets 5 minutes. Remove to wire racks; cool completely.

7. Add food coloring, a few drops at a time, to frosting; stir until evenly tinted. Spread medium circles with frosting. Let stand 10 minutes or until set. Spread thin layer of frosting on backs of medium circles and adhere to large circles for mouth. Cut lengths of licorice for noses and mouths; press into frosting.

8. Spread small circle of frosting on inside of each small circle for ears. Dot backs of 2 candies with frosting; adhere to each large circle just above medium circle for eyes. Let stand 10 minutes or until set.

Mischievous Monkeys

Makin' Bacon Cookies

Makes about 2 dozen cookies

1 package (about 16 ounces) refrigerated
   break-apart sugar cookie dough
   (24 count)

½ cup water, divided
Red, brown and yellow gel
   food colorings

1. Let dough stand at room temperature 5 minutes. Lightly grease or line cookie sheets with parchment paper.

2. Preheat oven to 325°F. Roll out dough between sheets of parchment paper to ¼-inch thickness. Cut out bacon shapes with sharp knife (approximately 3½×1-inch shapes). Place 2 inches apart on prepared cookie sheets. Refrigerate 15 minutes.

3. Bake 13 minutes or until set. Cool on cookie sheets 5 minutes. Remove to wire racks; cool completely.

4. Place ¼ cup water in small bowl. Add red and brown food colorings, a few drops at a time; stir until evenly tinted. Place remaining ¼ cup water in another small bowl. Add red and yellow food colorings, a few drops at a time; stir until evenly tinted. Paint cookies to resemble bacon with small clean paintbrushes,* using as little water as possible for color to saturate. Leave some areas unpainted to resemble bacon fat. Let stand 1 hour or until dry.

Do not use paintbrushes that have been used for anything other than food.

Tip

To make your own custom-designed cutout cookies, cut a simple bacon shape out of clean, heavy cardboard or poster board. Place the cardboard pattern on the rolled out cookie dough and cut around it using a sharp knife.

Makin' Bacon Cookies

Snapshot Cookies
Makes 1 dozen cookies

3½ cups all-purpose flour
1 teaspoon salt
1½ cups sugar
1 cup (2 sticks) unsalted butter, softened
2 eggs

2 teaspoons vanilla
Royal Icing (page 128)
Black gel food coloring
Assorted colored round candies
12 mini gummy candies

1. Whisk flour and salt in medium bowl. Beat sugar and butter in large bowl with electric mixer at medium speed until light and fluffy. Add eggs, one at a time, beating well after each addition. Add vanilla; beat until blended.

2. Gradually add flour mixture, beating well after each addition. Divide dough in half; shape each half into disc. Wrap and refrigerate 1 hour or until chilled.

3. Preheat oven to 350°F. Lightly grease or line cookie sheets with parchment paper.

4. Working with one disc at a time, roll out dough between sheets of parchment paper to ¼-inch thickness. From each disc, cut out 6 rectangles with sharp knife (approximately 2½×3½-inch shapes) and 6 circles with 1½-inch round cookie cutter.

5. Place rectangles 2 inches apart on prepared cookie sheets. Place circles 1 inch apart on separate prepared cookie sheet. Refrigerate 15 minutes.

6. Bake rectangles 15 minutes or until set. Bake circles 12 minutes or until set. Cool on cookie sheets 5 minutes. Remove to wire racks; cool completely.

7. Prepare Royal Icing. Reserve 1 cup Royal Icing. Add food coloring, a few drops at a time, to remaining icing; stir until evenly tinted. Spread rectangles with black icing. Let stand 10 minutes or until set. Spread circles with reserved white icing. Spread thin layer of white icing on back of circles and adhere to rectangles for lens. Let stand 10 minutes or until set.

8. Dot back of candies with icing and adhere for flash, viewfinder and lens. Dot back of gummy candy with icing and adhere to side of rectangle for button. Let stand 10 minutes or until set.

Snapshot Cookies

Sparkling Magic Wands
Makes 4 dozen cookies

1 package (18 ounces) refrigerated sugar
    cookie dough
48 pretzel sticks (2½ inches long)

Colored decorating icings
Colored sugar and gold dragées

1. Preheat oven to 350°F.

2. Roll out dough between sheets of parchment paper to ¼-inch thickness. Cut out shapes with 2-inch star cookie cutter. Place each star on top of one pretzel stick; press lightly to attach. Place on ungreased cookie sheet.

3. Bake 5 minutes or until edges are lightly browned. Cool on cookie sheet 2 minutes. Remove to wire racks; cool completely.

4. Spread icing on stars; sprinkle with colored sugar. Press dragées onto points of stars. Let stand until set.

Marshmallow Ice Cream Cone Cookies
Makes 1½ dozen cookies

1 package (about 16 ounces) refrigerated
    sugar cookie dough
6 ice cream sugar cones, broken into pieces
1 container (16 ounces) white frosting

1 package (about 10 ounces) colored
    mini marshmallows
Colored sprinkles

1. Let dough stand at room temperature 15 minutes. Preheat oven to 350°F.

2. Place sugar cones in food processor. Process using on/off pulsing action until finely ground. Combine dough and sugar cones in large bowl; beat until well blended.

3. Shape dough into 3 equal balls. Pat each ball into 9-inch circle on lightly floured surface. Cut each circle into 6 wedges; place 2 inches apart on ungreased cookie sheets.

4. Bake 10 minutes or until edges are lightly browned. While cookies are still warm, score crisscross pattern into cookies. Cool on cookie sheets 5 minutes. Remove to wire racks; cool completely.

5. Spread 2-inch strip of frosting at wide end of each cookie. Press marshmallows into frosting; top with sprinkles.

Sparkling Magic Wands

Swashbuckling Pirates

Makes about 1½ dozen cookies

3½ cups all-purpose flour
1 teaspoon salt
1½ cups sugar
1 cup (2 sticks) unsalted butter, softened
2 eggs
2 teaspoons vanilla
Royal Icing (page 128)

Pink, orange, yellow and red gel food colorings
Red string licorice
Red candy-coated chocolate pieces
Black decorating gel
Mini semisweet chocolate chips

1. Whisk flour and salt in medium bowl. Beat sugar and butter in large bowl with electric mixer at medium speed until light and fluffy. Add eggs, one at a time, beating well after each addition. Add vanilla; beat until blended.

2. Gradually add flour mixture, beating well after each addition. Divide dough in half; shape each half into disc. Wrap and refrigerate 1 hour.

3. Preheat oven to 350°F. Lightly grease or line cookie sheets with parchment paper.

4. Working with one disc at a time, roll out dough between sheets of parchment paper to ¼-inch thickness. Cut out circles with 3¼-inch round cookie cutter. Place 1 inch apart on prepared cookie sheets. Refrigerate 15 minutes.

5. Bake 15 minutes or until set. Cool on cookie sheets 5 minutes. Remove to wire racks; cool completely.

6. Prepare Royal Icing. Reserve one third of icing in small bowl. Add pink, orange and yellow food colorings, a few drops at a time, to remaining icing to create peach color; stir until evenly tinted. Spread two thirds of each cookie with peach icing. Let stand 10 minutes or until set.

7. Spread remaining one third of each cookie with reserved white icing. Cut licorice for edge of bandana and mouth; press into icing. Press chocolate pieces into white icing. Let stand 10 minutes or until set.

8. Pipe eye patch using decorating gel. Pipe eye with white icing; press mini chocolate chip into center of eye. Press mini chocolate chips into icing for mustache. Let stand 10 minutes or until set.

Mighty Milk Shakes
Makes 1½ dozen brownies

1 package (about 19 ounces) brownie mix, plus ingredients to prepare mix

1 package (14 ounces) milk chocolate or peanut butter candy discs

½ (16-ounce) container white or vanilla frosting

Colored drinking straws

Colored sprinkles

1. Preheat oven to 350°F. Coat 9-inch square baking pan with nonstick cooking spray.

2. Prepare brownie mix according to package directions; pour batter into prepared pan. Bake 35 minutes or until toothpick inserted into center comes out clean. Cool completely in pan on wire rack. Cover; freeze 1 hour or overnight.

3. Run knife around edges of brownies. Place cutting board over baking pan; invert and let stand until brownies release from pan. Trim edges; discard. Cut into 18 rectangles.

4. Place candy discs in medium microwavable bowl. Microwave on HIGH 1 minute; stir. If necessary, microwave at additional 15-second intervals until smooth and spreadable. Stand brownies up on small side. Spread all sides with candy mixture. Let stand on wire racks 10 minutes or until set.

5. Pipe frosting on top of each brownie for whipped cream. Decorate with straws and sprinkles.

Mighty Milk Shakes

Panda Pals
Makes 1 dozen cookies

3½ cups all-purpose flour
1 teaspoon salt
1½ cups sugar
1 cup (2 sticks) unsalted butter, softened
2 eggs

1 teaspoon almond extract
1 teaspoon vanilla
1 cup prepared white or vanilla frosting
Black gel food coloring
Black jelly beans, cut in half

1. Whisk flour and salt in medium bowl. Beat sugar and butter in large bowl with electric mixer at medium speed until light and fluffy. Add eggs, one at a time, beating well after each addition. Add almond extract and vanilla; beat until blended.

2. Gradually add flour mixture, beating well after each addition. Divide dough in half; shape each half into disc. Wrap and refrigerate 1 hour.

3. Preheat oven to 350°F. Lightly grease or line cookie sheets with parchment paper.

4. Working with one disc at a time, roll out dough between sheets of parchment paper to ¼-inch thickness. From each disc, cut out 6 large circles with 3-inch round cookie cutter, 6 medium circles with 1¾-inch round cookie cutter and 12 small circles with 1¼-inch round cookie cutter.

5. Place large circles 3 inches apart on prepared cookie sheets. Place 2 small circles next to each large circle for ears. Place medium circles 1 inch apart on separate prepared cookie sheet. Refrigerate 15 minutes.

6. Bake large circles 15 minutes or until set. Bake medium circles 12 minutes or until set. Cool on cookie sheets 5 minutes. Remove to wire racks; cool completely.

7. Spread medium circles with frosting; spread thin layer of frosting on backs and adhere to large circles for mouth. Add food coloring, a few drops at a time, to remaining frosting; stir until evenly tinted. Spread small circles with black frosting for ears. Pipe mouth using black frosting. Dot cut side of jelly beans with frosting and adhere for eyes and noses. Let stand 10 minutes or until set.

Panda Pals

Heart Cookie Pops

Makes 2 dozen cookie pops

1 package (about 18 ounces) red velvet or
    strawberry cake mix with pudding in
    the mix
½ cup (1 stick) butter, melted
2 eggs, lightly beaten
2 tablespoons honey

24 paper lollipop sticks
Prepared frosting
Valentine candy decorations
    and sprinkles

1. Combine cake mix, butter, eggs and honey in large bowl until well blended. Cover; refrigerate 30 minutes.

2. Preheat oven to 375°F. Lightly grease or line cookie sheets with parchment paper.

3. Shape dough by tablespoonfuls into 1-inch balls. Press 2 balls of dough together and taper bottom to form point of heart. Place heart on top of lollipop stick; press lightly to attach. Place 2 inches apart on prepared cookie sheets.

4. Bake 10 minutes or until edges are lightly browned. Cool on cookie sheets 3 minutes. Remove to wire racks; cool completely.

5. Frost cookies; decorate with candy and sprinkles.

Heart Cookie Pops

Building Blocks
Makes about 2½ dozen cookies

1 package (about 16 ounces) refrigerated
   cookie dough, any flavor
Powdered Sugar Glaze (recipe follows)

Assorted food colorings
Assorted small round gummy candies
   (about ¼ inch in diameter)

1. Let dough stand at room temperature 15 minutes. Grease 13×9-inch baking pan.

2. Preheat oven to 350°F. Press dough evenly into bottom of prepared pan. Score dough lengthwise and crosswise into 32 equal rectangles (about 2¼×1½ inches each). Freeze 10 minutes.

3. Bake 10 minutes. Re-score partially baked cookies. Bake 5 minutes or until edges are lightly browned and center is set. Cut through score marks to separate cookies. Cool in pan 10 minutes. Remove to wire racks; cool completely.

4. Prepare Powdered Sugar Glaze. Tint glaze with food colorings as desired.

5. Place wire racks over waxed paper. Spread glaze over tops and sides of cookies. Let stand 5 minutes. Attach 6 gummy candies to each cookie. Let stand 40 minutes or until set.

Powdered Sugar Glaze
Makes about 1 cup glaze

2 cups powdered sugar
6 to 9 tablespoons whipping cream,
   divided

1 teaspoon vanilla

Combine powdered sugar, 6 tablespoons cream and vanilla in medium bowl; whisk until smooth. Add enough remaining cream, 1 tablespoon at a time, to make pourable glaze.

Building Blocks

Magic Number Cookies

Makes about 1 dozen cookies

3½ cups all-purpose flour
1 teaspoon salt
1½ cups sugar
1 cup (2 sticks) unsalted butter, softened

2 eggs
2 teaspoons vanilla
Fuchsia and teal gel food colorings

1. Whisk flour and salt in medium bowl. Beat sugar and butter in large bowl with electric mixer at medium speed until light and fluffy. Add eggs, one at a time, beating well after each addition. Add vanilla; beat until blended.

2. Gradually add flour mixture, beating well after each addition. Divide dough in half; place in separate medium bowls. Add fuchsia food coloring, a few drops at a time, to half of dough; beat until evenly tinted. Add teal food coloring, a few drops at a time, to remaining half of dough; beat until evenly tinted. Shape each half of dough into disc. Wrap and refrigerate 1 hour.

3. Preheat oven to 350°F. Lightly grease or line cookie sheets with parchment paper.

4. Working with one disc at a time, roll out dough between sheets of parchment paper to ¼-inch thickness. Cut out stars with 4½-inch and 3½-inch cookie cutters. Place 1 inch apart on prepared cookie sheets. Cut out number from center of each star using 2-inch and ½-inch cookie cutters. Transfer fuchsia numbers to teal stars and teal numbers to fuchsia stars. Refrigerate 15 minutes.

5. Bake 15 minutes or until set. Cool on cookie sheets 5 minutes. Remove to wire racks; cool completely.

Magic Number Cookies

Silly Sunglasses

Makes about 1 dozen cookies

3½ cups all-purpose flour
1 teaspoon salt
1½ cups sugar
1 cup (2 sticks) unsalted butter, softened
2 eggs

2 teaspoons vanilla
24 to 32 fruit-flavored hard candies, crushed
Assorted colored decorating icings and decors

1. Whisk flour and salt in medium bowl. Beat sugar and butter in large bowl with electric mixer at medium speed until light and fluffy. Add eggs, one at a time, beating well after each addition. Add vanilla; beat until blended.

2. Gradually add flour mixture, beating well after each addition. Divide dough in half; shape each half into disc. Wrap and refrigerate 1 hour.

3. Preheat oven to 350°F. Lightly grease or line cookie sheets with parchment paper.

4. Working with one disc at a time, roll out dough between sheets of parchment paper to ¼-inch thickness. Cut out sunglasses with sharp knife (approximately 4×2-inch shapes). Place 2 inches apart on prepared cookie sheets. Cut out lenses from sunglasses; reroll scraps to make additional sunglasses. Refrigerate 15 minutes.

5. Sprinkle crushed candy into each lens opening. Bake 8 minutes or until candy is melted and cookies are set. Cool completely on cookie sheets. Decorate with icings and decors as desired.

Silly Sunglasses

Snickerpoodles
Makes about 2 dozen cookies

1 package (about 16 ounces) refrigerated
    sugar cookie dough
1 teaspoon ground cinnamon, divided
1 teaspoon vanilla

¼ cup sugar
Semisweet chocolate chips
Mini semisweet chocolate chips
White and pink decorating icings

1. Let dough stand at room temperature 15 minutes. Lightly grease or line cookie sheets with parchment paper.

2. Preheat oven to 350°F. Combine dough, ½ teaspoon cinnamon and vanilla in large bowl; beat with electric mixer at medium speed until well blended. Combine sugar and remaining ½ teaspoon cinnamon in small bowl.

3. Shape 1½ teaspoonful dough into oval for face. Roll in cinnamon-sugar; place on prepared cookie sheets. Divide 1½ teaspoonful dough in half; shape each half into teardrop shape. Roll in cinnamon-sugar; place at either side of face. Shape scant teaspoonful dough into oval. Roll in cinnamon-sugar; place at top of face. Repeat with remaining dough and cinnamon-sugar.

4. Bake 10 minutes or until edges are lightly browned. Immediately press 1 chocolate chip onto each face for nose. Cool on cookie sheets 2 minutes. Remove to wire racks; cool completely.

5. Pipe two small circles on each face with white decorating icing. Press mini chocolate chips into icing for eyes. Decorate as desired with white and pink icings.

Snickerpoodles

Holiday Delights

Window-to-My-Heart Cookies
Makes about 3 dozen cookies

2¼ cups all-purpose flour
½ teaspoon salt
¼ teaspoon baking powder
1 cup (2 sticks) butter, softened
½ cup powdered sugar

¼ cup packed brown sugar
1 teaspoon vanilla
1 cup dried cranberries, chopped
15 to 20 cherry- or cinnamon-flavored hard candies, crushed

1. Whisk flour, salt and baking powder in medium bowl. Beat butter, powdered sugar, brown sugar and vanilla in large bowl with electric mixer at medium speed until light and fluffy. Gradually add flour mixture, beating well after each addition. Stir in cranberries. Shape dough into disc. Wrap and refrigerate 1 hour.

2. Preheat oven to 325°F. Lightly grease or line cookie sheets with parchment paper.

3. Roll out dough between sheets of parchment paper to ¼-inch thickness. Cut out shapes using 2- to 3-inch heart cookie cutter. Cut out center of each cookie using smaller heart cookie cutter; re-roll scraps to make additional hearts. Place 1 inch apart on prepared cookie sheets. Sprinkle crushed candy into each center.

4. Bake 20 minutes or until candy is melted and cookies are set. Remove to wire racks; cool completely.

Snowpeople Cookies
Makes 1 dozen cookies

2¼ cups all-purpose flour

½ teaspoon baking soda

1 package (8 ounces) cream cheese, softened

1 cup powdered sugar

½ cup (1 stick) unsalted butter, softened

½ teaspoon almond extract

Additional powdered sugar

12 sticks red or striped chewing gum

Mini candy-coated chocolate pieces

Red gummy candies, flattened and trimmed

Decorating icing

1. Preheat oven to 325°F. Lightly grease or line cookie sheets with parchment paper.

2. Whisk flour and baking soda in medium bowl. Beat cream cheese, 1 cup powdered sugar, butter and almond extract in large bowl with electric mixer at medium speed until well blended.

3. Shape dough into equal number of ½-inch, 1-inch and 1½-inch diameter balls. Using one small, medium and large ball per snowperson, place balls nearly touching on prepared cookie sheets. Flatten each ball to ¼-inch thickness using bottom of glass dipped in flour.

4. Bake 15 minutes or until edges are lightly browned. Cool on cookie sheets 1 minute. Remove to wire racks; cool completely.

5. Sprinkle each snowperson with additional powdered sugar. Using one stick of gum, make scarf with fringed ends for each snowperson. Use chocolate pieces for eyes and gummy candies for mouths, securing with decorating icing.

Snowpeople Cookies

Easter Nest Cookies

Makes about 3½ dozen cookies

1½ cups all-purpose flour
1 teaspoon baking powder
½ teaspoon salt
¾ cup (1½ sticks) butter
2 cups miniature marshmallows
½ cup sugar
1 egg white

1 teaspoon vanilla extract
½ teaspoon almond extract
3¾ cups MOUNDS® Sweetened
   Coconut Flakes, divided
JOLLY RANCHER® Jelly Beans
HERSHEY®S Candy-Coated Milk
   Chocolate Eggs

1. Heat oven to 375°F.

2. Stir together flour, baking powder and salt; set aside. Place butter and marshmallows in microwave-safe bowl. Microwave at HIGH (100%) 1 to 1½ minutes or just until mixture melts when stirred. Beat sugar, egg white, vanilla and almond extract in separate bowl; add melted butter mixture, beating until light and fluffy. Gradually add flour mixture, beating until blended. Stir in 2 cups coconut.

3. Shape dough into 1-inch balls; roll balls in remaining 1¾ cups coconut, tinting coconut, if desired.* Place balls on ungreased cookie sheet. Press thumb into center of each ball, creating shallow depression.

4. Bake 8 to 10 minutes or just until lightly browned. Place 1 to 3 jelly beans and milk chocolate eggs in center of each cookie. Transfer to wire rack; cool completely.

To tint coconut: Place ¾ teaspoon water and a few drops food color in small bowl; stir in 1¾ cups coconut. Toss with fork until evenly tinted; cover tightly.

Easter Nest Cookies

Christmas Clouds
Makes 2½ dozen cookies

2 cups all-purpose flour
1 cup finely chopped pecans
1 teaspoon ground cinnamon

1 cup (2 sticks) unsalted butter, softened
1 cup powdered sugar, divided
1 teaspoon vanilla

1. Preheat oven to 350°F.

2. Combine flour, pecans and cinnamon in medium bowl. Beat butter, ½ cup powdered sugar and vanilla in large bowl with electric mixer at medium speed until light and fluffy. Gradually add flour mixture, beating at low speed until blended after each addition. (Dough will be stiff and crumbly.)

3. Shape dough by tablespoonfuls into 1-inch balls; place 2 inches apart on ungreased cookie sheets.

4. Bake 15 minutes or until bottoms are lightly browned. Cool on cookie sheets 5 minutes. Gently roll warm cookies in remaining ½ cup powdered sugar. Remove to wire racks; cool completely.

Rum Fruitcake Cookies
Makes about 6 dozen cookies

1 cup sugar
¾ cup (¾ stick) shortening
3 eggs
⅓ cup orange juice
1 tablespoon rum extract

3 cups all-purpose flour
2 teaspoons baking powder
1 teaspoon *each* baking soda and salt
2 cups (8 ounces) chopped candied fruit
1 cup *each* chopped nuts and raisins

1. Preheat oven to 375°F. Lightly grease or line cookie sheets with parchment paper.

2. Beat sugar and shortening in large bowl with electric mixer at medium speed until light and fluffy. Add eggs, orange juice and rum extract; beat 2 minutes. Combine flour, baking powder, baking soda and salt in medium bowl. Add candied fruit, nuts and raisins. Stir into shortening mixture.

3. Drop dough by rounded teaspoonfuls 2 inches apart onto prepared cookie sheets.

4. Bake 10 minutes or until lightly browned. Cool on cookie sheets 2 minutes. Remove to wire racks; cool completely.

Christmas Clouds

Masquerade Party Cookies

Makes 20 cookies

1 package (about 16 ounces) refrigerated
    chocolate chip cookie dough
¼ cup all-purpose flour

Colored nonpareils or sprinkles
Black decorating icing
Red string licorice, cut into 5-inch lengths

1. Let dough stand at room temperature 15 minutes. Lightly grease or line cookie sheets with parchment paper.

2. Preheat oven to 350°F. Beat dough and flour in large bowl with electric mixer at medium speed until well blended.

3. Shape dough into 20 (3-inch long) ovals; roll in nonpareils. Place 2 inches apart on prepared cookie sheets; flatten slightly. Pinch ovals in at centers to create mask shapes. Decorate with additional nonpareils.

4. Bake 8 minutes or until edges are lightly browned. Make oval indentations for eyes with back of spoon. Reshape at centers, if necessary. Cool completely on cookie sheets.

5. Spread eye area with icing. Attach licorice piece to each side of mask with icing. Let stand 15 minutes or until set.

Tip

For even baking and browning of cookies, bake them in the center of the oven. If the heat distribution in your oven is uneven, turn the cookie sheet halfway through baking time. Most cookies bake quickly and should be watched carefully to avoid overbaking. It is generally better to slightly underbake rather than overbake cookies.

Masquerade Party Cookies

Peppermint Snowballs

Makes 2 dozen snowballs

1½ cups sweetened shredded coconut
½ cup finely crushed peppermint candies*
¼ cup (½ stick) unsalted butter
4 cups mini marshmallows

½ teaspoon peppermint extract (optional)
5 cups crispy rice breakfast cereal
Vegetable oil

*About 18 peppermint candies will yield ½ cup finely crushed peppermints. To crush, place unwrapped candy in a heavy-duty resealable food storage bag. Loosely seal the bag, leaving an opening for air to escape. Crush with a rolling pin, meat mallet or the bottom of a heavy skillet.

1. Combine coconut and crushed candies in shallow pan.

2. Melt butter in large heavy saucepan over low heat. Add marshmallows; cook and stir until melted. Remove from heat. (Or place butter and marshmallows in large microwavable bowl. Microwave on HIGH at 30-second intervals, stirring between each interval until melted and smooth.)

3. While mixture is still warm, gently mix in peppermint extract, if desired, and rice cereal, stirring until well coated. With lightly oiled fingers, shape mixture into 24 (2-inch) balls. Roll balls in coconut mixture. Let stand until cool.

Tip: Snowballs can be frozen in resealable food storage bags or layered in an airtight container between sheets of waxed paper.

Peppermint Snowballs

Citrus Easter Chicks

Makes about 1½ dozen cookies

1 package (about 16 ounces) refrigerated
    sugar cookie dough
⅓ cup all-purpose flour
1 teaspoon lemon extract

Lemon Cookie Glaze (recipe follows)
2 cups flaked coconut, tinted yellow*
    Mini semisweet chocolate chips, assorted
    candies and decors

*To tint coconut, combine small amount of food coloring (paste or liquid) with 1 teaspoon water in large
bowl. Add coconut and stir until evenly coated. Add more food coloring, if necessary.*

1. Let dough stand at room temperature 15 minutes.

2. Beat dough, flour and lemon extract in large bowl with electric mixer at medium speed until well
blended. Divide dough in half; shape each half into disc. Wrap and refrigerate 1 hour.

3. Preheat oven to 350°F. Working with one disc at a time, roll out dough between sheets of
parchment paper to ¼-inch thickness. Cut out shapes with 2- to 3-inch chick cookie cutters. Place
2 inches apart on ungreased cookie sheets.

4. Bake 8 minutes or until set. Cool on cookie sheets 5 minutes. Remove to wire racks; cool
completely.

5. Place wire racks over parchment paper. Prepare Lemon Cookie Glaze; spread over cookies.
Sprinkle with coconut. Decorate chicks with chocolate chips, candies and decors as desired.
Let stand 40 minutes or until set.

Lemon Cookie Glaze

Makes about 2 cups glaze

4 cups powdered sugar
½ teaspoon grated lemon peel

4 to 6 tablespoons lemon juice
Yellow food coloring

Combine powdered sugar, lemon peel and lemon juice, 1 tablespoon at a time, in medium bowl to
make pourable glaze. Add food coloring, a few drops at a time; stir until evenly tinted.

Citrus Easter Chicks

Cornucopia Crunchers

Makes about 1 dozen cookies

¼ cup (½ stick) plus 1 tablespoon unsalted butter

½ cup packed dark brown sugar

1 egg

¼ cup all-purpose flour

½ teaspoon vanilla

Dash salt

⅓ cup finely chopped roasted macadamia nuts

Candy corn, mixed nuts or other Halloween candies

1. Preheat oven to 375°F. Lightly grease or line cookie sheets with parchment paper.

2. Beat butter and brown sugar in medium bowl with electric mixer at medium-high speed until light and fluffy. Add egg, flour, vanilla and salt; beat until blended. Stir in macadamia nuts.

3. Drop batter by rounded tablespoonfuls onto prepared cookie sheets. Arrange 6 cookies per sheet, flattening to 2-inch discs. (Cookies will spread to about 6 inches and become very lacy while baking.)

4. Bake 6 minutes or until lightly browned. Cool on cookie sheets 1 minute. Working quickly with spatula, ease one cookie at a time from cookie sheet. Keeping top of cookie on the outside, form into cornucopia shape by hand, or by partially wrapping around handle of wooden spoon. Place cornucopia, seam side down, on plate to harden. Repeat with remaining cookies. Return cookies to oven for 30 seconds, if necessary, to make them more pliable. Cool completely.

5. Fill cornucopias with candy corn and mixed nuts.

Note: For best results, use insulated light-colored cookie sheets. Thoroughly cool cookie sheets between batches.

Cornucopia Crunchers

Hanukkah Cookies

Makes 3½ dozen cookies

½ cup (1 stick) unsalted butter, softened

½ cup sugar

1 package (3 ounces) cream cheese, softened

¼ cup honey

1 egg

½ teaspoon vanilla

2½ cups all-purpose flour

⅓ cup finely ground walnuts

1 teaspoon baking powder

¼ teaspoon salt

Blue, white and yellow decorating icings

1. Beat butter, sugar, cream cheese, honey, egg and vanilla in large bowl with electric mixer at medium speed until light and fluffy. Stir in flour, walnuts, baking powder and salt until well blended. Divide dough in half; shape each half into disc. Wrap and refrigerate 2 hours or until firm.

2. Preheat oven to 350°F. Lightly grease or line cookie sheets with parchment paper.

3. Working with one disc at a time, roll out dough between sheets of parchment paper to ¼-inch thickness. Cut out shapes with 2½-inch dreidel and 6-pointed star cookie cutters. Place 2 inches apart on prepared cookie sheets.

4. Bake 8 minutes or until edges are lightly browned. Cool on cookie sheets 2 minutes. Remove to wire racks; cool completely. Decorate as desired with blue, white and yellow icings.

Tip

Unbaked cookie dough can be refrigerated for up to two weeks or frozen for up to six weeks. Label the dough with baking information for added convenience.

Hanukkah Cookies

Gobbler Cookies
Makes 1 dozen cookies

1 package (about 16 ounces) refrigerated
sugar cookie dough
¼ cup all-purpose flour
2 teaspoons ground cinnamon

Red, yellow, orange and white decorating
icings
Chocolate sprinkles, mini chocolate chips
and red string licorice

1. Let dough stand at room temperature 15 minutes. Preheat oven to 350°F. Lightly grease or line cookie sheets with parchment paper.

2. Beat dough, flour and cinnamon in large bowl with electric mixer at medium speed until well blended.

3. Shape dough into 12 large (1½-inch) balls, 12 medium (1-inch) balls and 12 small (¾-inch) balls.

4. Flatten large balls into 4-inch rounds on prepared cookie sheets; freeze 10 minutes. Bake 10 minutes or until lightly browned. Cool on cookie sheets 2 minutes. Remove to wire racks; cool completely.

5. Flatten medium balls into 2¼-inch rounds on prepared cookie sheets; freeze 10 minutes. Bake 8 minutes or until lightly browned. Cool on cookie sheets 2 minutes. Remove to wire racks; cool completely.

6. Flatten small balls into 1-inch rounds on prepared cookie sheets; freeze 10 minutes. Bake 6 minutes or until lightly browned. Cool on cookie sheets 2 minutes. Remove to wire racks; cool completely.

7. Decorate large cookies with red, yellow and orange icings and chocolate sprinkles to create feathers. Arrange medium cookies on large cookies towards bottom; place small cookies directly above medium cookies. Decorate turkeys with icings, chocolate chips and licorice for eyes, beaks, wattles and feet. Let stand 20 minutes or until set.

Buche de Noel Cookies

Makes about 2½ dozen cookies

⅔ cup butter or margarine, softened
1 cup granulated sugar
2 eggs
2 teaspoons vanilla extract
2½ cups all-purpose flour

½ cup HERSHEY'S Cocoa
½ teaspoon baking soda
¼ teaspoon salt
Mocha Frosting (recipe follows)
Powdered sugar (optional)

1. Beat butter and granulated sugar with electric mixer on medium speed in large bowl until well blended. Add eggs and vanilla; beat until fluffy. Stir together flour, cocoa, baking soda and salt; gradually add to butter mixture, beating until well blended. Cover; refrigerate dough 1 to 2 hours.

2. Heat oven to 350°F. Shape heaping teaspoons of dough into logs about 2½ inches long and ¾ inches in diameter; place on ungreased cookie sheet. Bake 7 to 9 minutes or until set. Cool slightly. Remove to wire rack and cool completely.

3. Frost cookies with Mocha Frosting. Using tines of fork, draw lines through frosting to imitate tree bark. Lightly dust with powdered sugar, if desired.

Mocha Frosting

Makes about 1⅔ cups frosting

6 tablespoons butter or margarine, softened
2⅔ cups powdered sugar
⅓ cup HERSHEY'S Cocoa
3 to 4 tablespoons milk

2 teaspoons powdered instant espresso powder dissolved in 1 teaspoon hot water
1 teaspoon vanilla extract

Beat butter with electric mixer on medium speed in medium bowl until creamy. Add powdered sugar and cocoa alternately with milk, dissolved espresso and vanilla, beating to spreadable consistency.

Jolly Peanut Butter Gingerbread Cookies

Makes about 6 dozen cookies

1⅔ cups (10-ounce package) REESE'S®
   Peanut Butter Chips
¾ cup (1½ sticks) butter or margarine,
   softened
1 cup packed light brown sugar
1 cup dark corn syrup
2 eggs

5 cups all-purpose flour
1 teaspoon baking soda
½ teaspoon ground cinnamon
¼ teaspoon ground ginger
¼ teaspoon salt

1. Place peanut butter chips in small microwave-safe bowl. Microwave at MEDIUM (50%) 1 minute; stir. If necessary, microwave at MEDIUM an additional 15 seconds at a time, stirring after each heating, until chips are melted when stirred. Beat melted peanut butter chips and butter in large bowl until well blended. Add brown sugar, corn syrup and eggs; beat until fluffy.

2. Stir together flour, baking soda, cinnamon, ginger and salt. Add half of flour mixture to butter mixture; beat on low speed of mixer until smooth. With wooden spoon, stir in remaining flour mixture until well blended. Divide into thirds; wrap each in plastic wrap. Refrigerate at least 1 hour or until dough is firm enough to roll.

3. Heat oven to 325°F. On lightly floured surface, roll 1 dough portion at a time to ⅛-inch thickness; cut into holiday shapes with floured cookie cutters. Place on ungreased cookie sheet.

4. Bake 10 to 12 minutes or until set and lightly browned. Cool slightly; remove from cookie sheet to wire rack. Cool completely. Frost and decorate as desired.

Jolly Peanut Butter Gingerbread Cookies

Earth Day Delights
Makes about 1½ dozen cookies

3½ cups all-purpose flour
1 teaspoon salt
1½ cups sugar
1 cup (2 sticks) unsalted butter, softened
2 eggs

2 teaspoons vanilla
1½ cups chopped pecans
Royal Icing (page 128)
Blue and green gel food colorings

1. Whisk flour and salt in medium bowl. Beat sugar and butter in large bowl with electric mixer at medium speed until light and fluffy. Add eggs, one at a time, beating well after each addition. Add vanilla; beat until blended.

2. Gradually add flour mixture, beating well after each addition. Stir in pecans. Divide dough in half; shape each half into disc. Wrap and refrigerate 1 hour.

3. Preheat oven to 350°F. Lightly grease or line cookie sheets with parchment paper.

4. Working with one disc at a time, roll out dough between sheets of parchment paper to ¼-inch thickness. Cut out circles with 3¼-inch round cookie cutter. Place 1 inch apart on prepared cookie sheets. Refrigerate 15 minutes.

5. Bake 15 minutes or until set. Cool on cookie sheets 5 minutes. Remove to wire racks; cool completely.

6. Prepare Royal Icing. Divide icing into two small bowls. Add blue food coloring to one bowl, a few drops at a time; stir until evenly tinted. Spread cookies with blue icing. Let stand 10 minutes or until set.

7. Add green food coloring to remaining bowl, a few drops at a time; stir until evenly tinted. Pipe continent shapes using green icing. Let stand 10 minutes or until set.

Earth Day Delights

Eggnog Cookies
Makes 4 dozen cookies

2¼ cups all-purpose flour
1 teaspoon baking powder
1 teaspoon ground cinnamon
1 teaspoon freshly grated nutmeg*
   or ground nutmeg
1¼ cups sugar

¾ cup (1½ sticks) unsalted butter, softened
½ cup eggnog (no alcohol added)
2 egg yolks
1 teaspoon vanilla
   Additional freshly grated nutmeg

Freshly grated nutmeg tastes much better than bottled ground nutmeg. Whole nutmeg seeds and mini graters are available in the supermarket spice section.

1. Preheat oven to 300°F.

2. Sift flour, baking powder, cinnamon and nutmeg onto waxed paper. Beat sugar and butter in large bowl with electric mixer at medium speed until light and fluffy. Beat in eggnog, egg yolks and vanilla. Gradually add flour mixture, beating at low speed until well blended.

3. Drop dough by rounded teaspoonfuls 2 inches apart onto ungreased cookie sheets. Sprinkle with additional nutmeg.

4. Bake 20 minutes or until bottoms are lightly browned. Cool on cookie sheets 2 minutes. Remove to wire racks; cool completely.

Eggnog Cookies

Peanut Butter Pumpkins

Makes about 2 dozen pumpkins

1 package (about 16 ounces) refrigerated
    peanut butter cookie dough
½ cup all-purpose flour
3 cups powdered sugar, sifted
4 to 5 tablespoons milk

Orange food coloring
Orange decorating sugar
Pretzel sticks
Green chewy fruit candies

1. Let dough stand at room temperature 15 minutes. Lightly grease or line cookie sheets with parchment paper.

2. Beat dough and flour in medium bowl with electric mixer at medium speed until well blended. Shape dough by tablespoonfuls into balls; place 2 inches apart on prepared cookie sheets. Freeze 20 minutes or until firm.

3. Press side of toothpick (not tip) into dough balls from top to bottom to create grooves. Press toothpick into top of each pumpkin to create hole for stem. Freeze 15 minutes. Preheat oven to 350°F.

4. Bake 12 minutes or until lightly browned. Immediately press toothpick into tops of pumpkins again for stem. Cool on cookie sheets 5 minutes. Remove to wire racks; cool completely.

5. Place wire racks over sheets of waxed paper. Place powdered sugar in medium bowl; whisk in milk until blended. (Glaze should be thick but pourable.) Add orange food coloring, a few drops at a time; stir until evenly tinted.

6. Holding bottoms of cookies, dip tops of cookies into glaze, turning to coat. Let excess glaze drip off before placing cookies right side up on wire racks. Sprinkle with decorating sugar. Break pretzel sticks into ½-inch pieces; insert into center holes for stems.

7. Press candies with palm of hand to flatten. (Candies can also be stretched with fingers.) Cut out small (¼-inch) leaf shapes with scissors. Arrange leaves around pretzel stems.

Peanut Butter Pumpkins

Festive Candy Canes
Makes about 2 dozen cookies

1 cup powdered sugar
¾ cup (1½ sticks) butter, softened
1 egg
1 teaspoon peppermint extract

½ teaspoon vanilla
1⅔ to 1¾ cups all-purpose flour
⅛ teaspoon salt
Red food coloring

1. Preheat oven to 350°F.

2. Beat powdered sugar and butter in large bowl with electric mixer at medium speed until light and fluffy. Add egg, peppermint extract and vanilla; beat until well blended. Add flour and salt; beat until well blended. (Dough will be sticky.)

3. Divide dough in half. Add red food coloring to half of dough, a few drops at a time; knead until evenly tinted. Leave remaining dough plain. For each candy cane, shape heaping teaspoonful of each color dough into 5-inch rope with floured hands. Twist together into candy cane shape. Place 2 inches apart on ungreased cookie sheets.

4. Bake 8 minutes or until set and edges are lightly browned. Cool on cookie sheets 2 minutes. Remove to wire racks; cool completely.

Festive Candy Canes

Bar Cookie Bonanza

Easy No-Bake Crunchy Cranberry Almond Bars
Makes 2 dozen bars

Nonstick cooking spray
4 cups miniature marshmallows
¼ cup (½ stick) butter
¼ teaspoon salt
2 cups (12-ounce package) NESTLÉ® TOLL HOUSE® Premier White Morsels, divided

4 cups toasted wheat cereal squares
¾ cup sweetened dried cranberries
¾ cup sliced almonds, toasted*

*To toast almonds, bake at 350°F until light golden brown, about 8 minutes, stirring frequently.

LINE 13×9-inch baking pan with foil leaving an overhang on two sides. Spray foil with nonstick cooking spray.

HEAT marshmallows, butter and salt in large, heavy-duty saucepan over medium-low heat, stirring frequently, for 5 to 10 minutes, until smooth. Remove from heat. Add *1 cup* morsels; stir until melted.

WORKING QUICKLY, stir in cereal, cranberries, almonds and *remaining 1 cup morsels*. Spread mixture into prepared baking pan with greased spatula, pressing down lightly. Cool for 2 hours or until set. Lift from pan; peel off foil. Cut into bars with serrated knife.

Autumn Pumpkin Bars
Makes about 1½ dozen bars

2 cups all-purpose flour
2 teaspoons pumpkin pie spice
1 teaspoon baking powder
½ teaspoon salt
¼ teaspoon baking soda
1 cup plus 2 tablespoons packed brown sugar

¾ cup (1½ sticks) butter, softened
1 egg
1½ cups solid-pack pumpkin
1 teaspoon vanilla
1 cup semisweet chocolate chips, melted

1. Preheat oven to 350°F. Grease 13×9-inch baking pan.

2. Whisk flour, pumpkin pie spice, baking powder, salt and baking soda in medium bowl. Beat brown sugar and butter in large bowl with electric mixer at medium speed 3 minutes or until light and fluffy. Beat in egg until blended. Beat in pumpkin and vanilla. (Mixture may look curdled.)

3. Gradually add flour mixture, beating at low speed just until blended after each addition. Spread batter evenly in prepared pan.

4. Bake 25 minutes or until toothpick inserted into center comes out clean. Cool completely in pan on wire rack.

5. Cut out pumpkin and leaf shapes with 2- to 3-inch cookie cutters. Place melted chocolate in small resealable food storage bag. Cut off small corner. Pipe veins on leaves and lines on pumpkins with chocolate.

Autumn Pumpkin Bars

Apricot Almond Bars

Makes 3 dozen bars

½ cup (1 stick) plus 2 tablespoons butter
⅓ cup granulated sugar
¾ teaspoon almond extract, divided
1½ cups all-purpose flour
⅛ teaspoon salt

½ cup apricot or any flavor preserves
½ cup powdered sugar
2 to 2½ teaspoons fresh lemon juice or water
¼ cup toasted almonds* (optional)

*To toast almonds, spread sliced almonds in a shallow pan. Bake at 350°F for about 5 minutes or until lightly browned. Almonds burn easily.

Beat butter, sugar and ½ teaspoon almond extract with an electric mixer until fluffy. Stir in flour and salt. Dough will be stiff. Divide into 4 sections. Roll each section into a 9-inch log. Space at least 3 inches apart on cookie sheet. Using side of finger or handle of a wooden spoon, make a groove down center of each log about halfway into the log.

Bake in 375°F preheated oven for 10 minutes. Remove from oven and fill the groove with preserves. Return to oven and bake an additional 6 to 8 minutes or until golden.

Combine powdered sugar, ¼ teaspoon almond extract and enough lemon juice or water to make a frosting that can be drizzled. Drizzle frosting over preserves while bars are still warm. Sprinkle immediately with almonds. Cut into 1-inch bars with a sharp knife.

Favorite recipe from **North Dakota Wheat Commission**

Apricot Almond Bars

Triple Peanut Butter Oatmeal Bars

Makes about 2½ dozen bars

1½ cups firmly packed brown sugar
1 cup peanut butter
½ cup (1 stick) margarine or butter, softened
2 large eggs
1 teaspoon vanilla
2 cups QUAKER® Oats (quick or old fashioned, uncooked)

1 cup all-purpose flour
½ teaspoon baking soda
1 bag (8 ounces) candy-coated peanut butter pieces
½ cup chopped peanuts

1. Heat oven to 350°F. Lightly spray 13×9-inch baking pan with nonstick cooking spray.

2. Beat brown sugar, peanut butter and margarine in large bowl with electric mixer until creamy. Add eggs and vanilla; beat well. Add combined oats, flour and baking soda; mix well. Stir in peanut butter pieces. Spread dough evenly into pan. Sprinkle with peanuts, pressing in lightly with fingers.

3. Bake 35 to 40 minutes or just until center is set. Cool completely on wire rack. Cut into bars. Store tightly covered.

Tangy Lemon Raspberry Bars

Makes 1 dozen bars

¾ cup packed light brown sugar
½ cup (1 stick) butter, softened
Grated peel of 1 lemon
1 cup all-purpose flour

1 cup old-fashioned oats
1 teaspoon baking powder
½ teaspoon salt
½ cup raspberry jam

1. Preheat oven to 350°F. Grease 8-inch square baking pan.

2. Beat brown sugar, butter and lemon peel in large bowl with electric mixer at medium speed until blended. Add flour, oats, baking powder and salt; beat at low speed until combined. Reserve ¼ cup mixture. Press remaining mixture into prepared pan. Spread jam over top; sprinkle with reserved crumb mixture.

3. Bake 25 minutes or until edges are lightly browned. Cool completely in pan on wire rack. Cut into bars.

Triple Peanut Butter Oatmeal Bars

Holiday Walnut Berry Bites

Makes 4 dozen bars

Cooking Spray
2½ cups all-purpose flour
1 cup (2 sticks) cold margarine, cut into pieces
½ cup confectioners' sugar
½ teaspoon salt
1⅓ cups KARO® Light Corn Syrup

4 eggs
1 cup sugar
3 tablespoons butter, melted
2 cups fresh or thawed frozen cranberries, coarsely chopped
1 cup walnuts, chopped
1 cup white chocolate chips

Preheat oven to 350°F. Spray 15×10×1-inch baking pan with cooking spray. In large bowl, beat flour, margarine, confectioners' sugar and salt at medium speed until mixture resembles coarse crumbs; press firmly and evenly into pan. Bake 20 minutes or until golden brown.

In large bowl, beat syrup, eggs, sugar and butter until well blended. Stir in cranberries and walnuts.

Spread mixture evenly over hot crust. Sprinkle white chocolate chips over top. Bake 25 to 30 minutes or until set. Cool completely on wire rack before cutting into bars.

Prep Time: 30 minutes • **Bake Time:** 45 to 50 minutes

Carrot-Spice Squares with Butterscotch Morsels

Makes 2 dozen bars

1½ cups matchstick-size carrots

¼ cup water

1 package (about 18 ounces) spice
cake mix

1 cup old-fashioned oats

¾ cup vegetable oil

2 eggs

¾ cup butterscotch morsels

½ cup flaked coconut

½ cup chopped pecans*

To toast pecans, spread in single layer on cookie sheet. Bake in preheated 350°F oven 8 to 10 minutes or until golden brown, stirring frequently. Cool completely.

1. Preheat oven to 350°F. Grease 13×9-inch baking pan.

2. Place carrots and water in microwavable bowl; cover with plastic wrap. Microwave on HIGH 2 minutes; stir. Microwave 1 minute or until carrots are tender. Drain.

3. Beat carrots, cake mix, oats, oil and eggs in medium bowl with electric mixer at medium speed until blended. Spoon batter into prepared pan. Bake 20 minutes or until toothpick inserted into center comes out almost clean.

4. Immediately after removing from oven, sprinkle with butterscotch morsels, coconut and pecans. Press down with rubber spatula. Cool completely in pan on wire rack. For best flavor, cover with foil and let stand overnight. Cut into bars.

Carrot-Spice Squares with Butterscotch Morsels

Chocolate Cashew Coconut Bars

Makes 2½ dozen bars

1⅓ cups all-purpose flour
½ cup packed dark brown sugar
½ teaspoon baking powder
⅛ teaspoon salt
¾ cup (1½ sticks) unsalted butter, cubed, divided
1⅔ cups (10 ounces) finely chopped bittersweet chocolate

¾ cup whipping cream
½ cup granulated sugar
1 teaspoon vanilla
2 eggs
1½ cups flaked coconut
1½ cups chopped cashews

1. Preheat oven to 350°F. Grease 13×9-inch baking pan.

2. Whisk flour, brown sugar, baking powder and salt in medium bowl; cut in ½ cup butter with pastry blender or two knives until mixture resembles coarse crumbs. Press into bottom of prepared pan. Bake 10 minutes or until set. Cool in pan on wire rack.

3. Place chocolate in medium bowl. Bring cream to a simmer in small heavy saucepan over medium-low heat. Pour over chocolate. Let stand 5 minutes; stir until smooth. Pour over crust. Refrigerate 15 minutes or until set.

4. Beat remaining ¼ cup butter in medium bowl with electric mixer at medium speed until light and fluffy. Add granulated sugar and vanilla; beat until blended. Add eggs, one at a time, beating well after each addition. Fold in coconut and cashews.

5. Spoon topping evenly over filling; gently spread over surface. Bake 25 minutes or until golden brown. Cool completely in pan on wire rack. Cut into bars.

Chocolate Cashew Coconut Bars

No-Oven Peanut Butter Squares
Makes 4 dozen bars

½ cup (1 stick) butter or margarine
2 cups powdered sugar
1½ cups NABISCO® Graham Cracker
  Crumbs

1 cup peanut butter
1½ packages (12 squares) BAKER'S®
  Semi-Sweet Chocolate

Microwave Directions

LINE 13×9-inch baking pan with REYNOLDS foil, with ends of foil extending over sides of pan. Set aside.

MELT butter in large microwaveable bowl on HIGH 45 seconds until melted. Add sugar, cracker crumbs and peanut butter; mix well. Spread into prepared pan.

MICROWAVE chocolate in microwaveable bowl on HIGH 1½ to 2 minutes or until melted, stirring after each minute. Cool slightly, then pour over peanut butter mixture in pan. Cool. Cut partially through dessert to mark 48 squares. Refrigerate 1 hour or until set. Lift from pan, using foil handles. Cut all the way through dessert into squares.

Prep Time: 10 minutes • **Total Time:** 1 hour 10 minutes (includes refrigerating)

Tip

To make thicker squares, reduce chocolate to 1 package (8 squares). Prepare recipe as directed, using 9-inch square baking pan. Cut into 24 squares to serve.

No-Oven Peanut Butter Squares

Piña Colada Cookie Bars
Makes 3 dozen bars

½ cup (1 stick) butter, melted
1½ cups graham cracker crumbs
1 can (14 ounces) sweetened condensed milk
2 tablespoons dark rum

2 cups white chocolate chips
1 cup flaked coconut
½ cup chopped macadamia nuts
½ cup chopped dried pineapple

1. Preheat oven to 350°F.

2. Pour butter into 13×9-inch baking pan, tilting pan to coat bottom. Sprinkle graham cracker crumbs evenly over butter. Blend sweetened condensed milk and rum in small bowl; pour over crumbs. Top with white chocolate chips, coconut, nuts and pineapple.

3. Bake 25 minutes or until edges are lightly browned. Cool completely in pan on wire rack. Cut into bars.

Championship Chocolate Chip Bars
Makes about 3 dozen bars

1½ cups all-purpose flour
½ cup packed light brown sugar
½ cup (1 stick) cold butter or margarine
2 cups (12-ounce package) HERSHEY₅S SPECIAL DARK® Chocolate Chips or HERSHEY₅S Semi-Sweet Chocolate Chips, divided

1 can (14 ounces) sweetened condensed milk (not evaporated milk)
1 egg, slightly beaten
1 teaspoon vanilla extract
1 cup chopped nuts

1. Heat oven to 350°F.

2. Stir together flour and brown sugar in medium bowl; cut in cold butter until crumbly. Stir in ½ cup chocolate chips; press mixture onto bottom of ungreased 13×9-inch baking pan. Bake 15 minutes.

3. Combine sweetened condensed milk, egg and vanilla in large bowl. Stir in remaining 1½ cups chips and nuts. Spread over hot baked crust. Bake 25 minutes or until golden. Cool completely in pan on wire rack. Cut into bars.

Piña Colada Cookie Bars

Autumn Apple Bars

Makes about 3 dozen bars

1 package (15 ounces) refrigerated pie
    crusts (2 crusts)
1 cup graham cracker crumbs
8 cups tart cooking apples, peeled and
    sliced ¼ inch thick (about 8 to
    10 medium apples)
1 cup plus 2 tablespoons granulated sugar,
    divided

2½ teaspoons ground cinnamon, divided
¼ teaspoon ground nutmeg
1 egg white
1 cup powdered sugar
1 to 2 tablespoons milk
½ teaspoon vanilla

1. Preheat oven to 350°F. Roll out 1 pie crust between sheets of parchment paper to 15×10-inch rectangle. Place on bottom of ungreased 15×10-inch jelly-roll pan.

2. Sprinkle graham cracker crumbs over dough; layer apple slices over crumbs. Combine 1 cup granulated sugar, 1½ teaspoons cinnamon and nutmeg in small bowl; sprinkle over apples.

3. Roll out remaining pie crust between sheets of parchment paper to 15×10-inch rectangle; place over apple layer. Beat egg white in small bowl until foamy; brush over top crust. Stir remaining 2 tablespoons granulated sugar and 1 teaspoon cinnamon in separate small bowl; sprinkle over crust. Bake 45 minutes or until lightly browned.

4. Combine powdered sugar, 1 tablespoon milk and vanilla in small bowl. Add additional milk, if necessary, until desired consistency is reached. Drizzle over top. Cut into bars.

Autumn Apple Bars

Chocolate Crumb Bars

Makes 2½ dozen bars

1 cup (2 sticks) butter or margarine,
    softened
1¾ cups all-purpose flour
½ cup granulated sugar
¼ teaspoon salt
2 cups (12-ounce package) NESTLÉ®
    TOLL HOUSE® Semi-Sweet Chocolate
    Morsels, divided

1 can (14 ounces) NESTLÉ® CARNATION®
    Sweetened Condensed Milk
1 teaspoon vanilla extract
1 cup chopped walnuts (optional)

PREHEAT oven to 350°F. Grease 13×9-inch baking pan.

BEAT butter in large mixer bowl until creamy. Beat in flour, sugar and salt until crumbly. With floured fingers, press 2 cups crumb mixture onto bottom of prepared baking pan; reserve remaining mixture.

BAKE for 10 to 12 minutes or until edges are golden brown.

COMBINE 1 cup morsels and sweetened condensed milk in small, *heavy-duty* saucepan. Warm over low heat, stirring until smooth. Stir in vanilla extract. Spread over hot crust.

STIR nuts and remaining morsels into reserved crumb mixture; sprinkle over chocolate filling. Bake for 25 to 30 minutes or until center is set. Cool in pan on wire rack.

Chocolate Crumb Bars

O'Henrietta Bars
Makes 2 dozen bars

Cooking Spray
½ cup (1 stick) butter or margarine, softened
½ cup packed brown sugar
½ cup KARO® Light or Dark Corn Syrup

1 teaspoon vanilla
3 cups quick oats, uncooked
½ cup (3 ounces) semisweet chocolate chips
¼ cup creamy peanut butter

1. Preheat oven to 350°F. Spray 8- or 9-inch square baking pan with cooking spray.

2. Beat butter, brown sugar, corn syrup and vanilla in large bowl with mixer at medium speed until smooth. Stir in oats. Press into prepared pan.

3. Bake 25 minutes or until center is barely firm. Cool on wire rack 5 minutes.

4. Sprinkle with chocolate chips; top with small spoonfuls of peanut butter. Let stand 5 minutes; spread peanut butter and chocolate over bars, swirling to marble.

5. Cool completely on wire rack before cutting. Cut into bars; refrigerate 15 minutes to set topping.

Easy Turtle Bars
Makes 2½ dozen bars

1 package (about 18 ounces) chocolate
  cake mix
½ cup (1 stick) butter, melted
¼ cup milk

1 cup (6 ounces) semisweet chocolate chips
1 cup chopped pecans
1 jar (12 ounces) caramel ice cream
  topping

1. Preheat oven to 350°F. Grease 13×9-inch baking pan.

2. Combine cake mix, butter and milk in large bowl until well blended. Spread half of batter in prepared pan.

3. Bake 8 minutes or until crust begins to form. Sprinkle chocolate chips and half of ½ cup pecans over crust. Drizzle with caramel topping. Drop spoonfuls of remaining batter over caramel; sprinkle with remaining ½ cup pecans.

4. Bake 18 minutes or until top springs back when lightly touched. (Caramel center will be soft.) Cool completely in pan on wire rack. Cut into bars.

O'Henrietta Bars

Lemon Iced Ambrosia Bars

Makes about 2½ dozen bars

1¾ cups all-purpose flour, divided
⅓ cup powdered sugar
¾ cup (1½ sticks) unsalted butter
2 cups packed light brown sugar
1 cup flaked coconut

1 cup finely chopped pecans
4 eggs, beaten
½ teaspoon baking powder
Lemon Icing (recipe follows)

1. Preheat oven to 350°F. Grease 13×9-inch baking pan.

2. Combine 1½ cups flour and powdered sugar in medium bowl; cut in butter with pastry blender or two knives until mixture resembles coarse crumbs. Press onto bottom of prepared pan; bake 15 minutes.

3. Meanwhile, combine remaining ¼ cup flour, brown sugar, coconut, pecans, eggs and baking powder in medium bowl; mix well. Spread evenly over baked crust; bake 20 minutes. Cool completely in pan on wire rack.

4. Prepare Lemon Icing; spread over filling. Cut into bars. Cover and refrigerate until ready to serve.

Lemon Icing: Stir together 2 cups powdered sugar, 3 tablespoons lemon juice and 2 tablespoons softened butter until smooth. Makes about ⅔ cup.

Lemon Iced Ambrosia Bars

Hawaiian Bars
Makes about 1½ dozen bars

1⅓ cups all-purpose flour
1 teaspoon baking powder
¼ teaspoon baking soda
¼ teaspoon salt
½ cup (1 stick) plus 2 tablespoons
    unsalted butter, cubed
1 teaspoon vanilla

2 eggs
1 cup packed dark brown sugar
¾ cup coarsely chopped salted
    macadamia nuts
¾ cup flaked coconut
⅓ cup granulated sugar

1. Preheat oven to 350°F. Grease 9-inch square baking pan.

2. Whisk flour, baking powder, baking soda and salt in medium bowl. Melt butter in large heavy saucepan over low heat. Remove from heat; stir in vanilla. Whisk in eggs, one at a time, beating well after each addition. Add flour mixture, brown sugar, nuts, coconut and granulated sugar; mix well. Spread batter in prepared pan.

3. Bake 30 minutes or until lightly browned. Cool completely in pan on wire rack. Cut into bars.

Note: Bars firm up and taste better the next day.

Hawaiian Bars

Oat and Apricot Bars
Makes 2 dozen bars

1½ cups all-purpose flour
1½ cups old-fashioned oats
1 cup packed brown sugar
1½ teaspoons ground cinnamon
½ teaspoon salt

½ teaspoon baking soda
½ cup vegetable oil
¼ cup apple juice
1 cup apricot preserves* or apricot fruit spread

*Or substitute seedless raspberry preserves.

1. Preheat oven to 325°F. Grease 13×9-inch baking pan.

2. Whisk flour, oats, brown sugar, cinnamon, salt and baking soda in large bowl. Combine oil and apple juice in small bowl. Add to flour mixture; stir just until moistened. Reserve 1¼ cups mixture; press remaining mixture evenly into prepared pan. Spread preserves over top. Sprinkle with reserved mixture.

3. Bake 35 minutes or until lightly browned. Cool completely in pan on wire rack. Cut into bars.

Tip
Bar cookies are some of the easiest cookies to make—simply mix the batter, spread in the pan and bake. These cookies are also quick to prepare since they bake all at once rather than in batches on a cookie sheet. Always use the pan size called for in the recipe. Substituting a different pan will affect the cookies' texture. A smaller pan will give the bars a more cakelike texture; a larger pan will produce a flatter bar with a drier texture.

Oat and Apricot Bars

Brownies & Blondies

Chocolate Chile Brownies with Spiced Frosting
Makes 9 brownies

Brownies
- 1 package (18 to 19 ounces) brownie mix, plus ingredients to prepare mix
- 1 can (4 ounces) ORTEGA® Fire-Roasted Diced Green Chiles,* undrained

Frosting
- 1 cup powdered sugar
- 1 tablespoon ORTEGA® Chili Seasoning Mix
- 1½ to 2 tablespoons milk

*For moister brownies with a stronger chile flavor, use 2 cans (4 ounces each) ORTEGA® Fire-Roasted Diced Green Chiles.

PREHEAT oven to 350°F. Line 8-inch square baking pan with aluminum foil, extending foil over sides of pan; lightly coat with nonstick cooking spray.

PREPARE brownies according to package directions. Stir in chiles; mix until well blended. Pour into prepared baking pan. Bake 25 to 30 minutes, or use time recommended on package. Cool on wire rack. Using foil "handles," remove from pan.

BLEND powdered sugar and seasoning mix in small bowl. Stir in milk, adding more if necessary, until desired consistency. Spread on brownies. Slice and serve.

Tip: For a special presentation, sprinkle shaved chocolate on the brownies before serving.

Prep Time: 10 minutes • **Start-to-Finish Time:** 1 hour

Double-Chocolate Pecan Brownies

Makes 9 brownies

¾ cup all-purpose flour
¾ cup unsweetened cocoa powder
½ cup CREAM OF WHEAT® Hot Cereal
    (Instant, 1-minute, 2½-minute or
    10-minute cook time), uncooked
½ teaspoon baking powder

1¼ cups sugar
½ cup (1 stick) butter, softened
2 eggs
1 teaspoon vanilla extract
½ cup semisweet chocolate chips
½ cup pecans, chopped

1. Preheat oven to 350°F. Line 8-inch square baking pan with foil, extending foil over sides of pan; spray with nonstick cooking spray. Combine flour, cocoa, Cream of Wheat and baking powder in medium bowl; set aside.

2. Cream sugar and butter in large mixing bowl with electric mixer at medium speed. Add eggs and vanilla; mix until well combined.

3. Gradually add Cream of Wheat mixture; mix well. Spread batter evenly in pan, using spatula. Sprinkle chocolate chips and pecans evenly over top.

4. Bake 35 minutes. Let stand 5 minutes. Lift brownies from pan using aluminum foil. Cool completely before cutting.

Tip: For an even more decadent dessert, drizzle caramel sauce over the warm brownies and serve with mint chocolate chip ice cream.

Prep Time: 15 minutes • Start-to-Finish Time: 1 hour

Double-Chocolate Pecan Brownies

Dulce de Leche Blondies

Makes about 3 dozen blondies

2 cups all-purpose flour
1 teaspoon baking soda
1 teaspoon salt
1 cup packed brown sugar
1 cup (2 sticks) unsalted butter, softened

2 eggs
1½ teaspoons vanilla
1 package (14 ounces) caramels, unwrapped
½ cup evaporated milk

1. Preheat oven to 350°F. Grease 13×9-inch baking pan.

2. Whisk flour, baking soda and salt in medium bowl. Beat brown sugar and butter in large bowl with electric mixer at medium speed until light and fluffy. Add eggs, one at a time, beating well after each addition. Beat in vanilla. Gradually add flour mixture; beat just until blended. Spread half of batter in prepared pan. Bake 8 minutes. Cool in pan on wire rack 5 minutes.

3. Meanwhile, melt caramels with evaporated milk in small nonstick saucepan over low heat; reserve 2 tablespoons. Pour remaining caramel mixture over baked bottom layer. Drop tablespoonfuls of remaining batter over caramel layer; swirl slightly with knife.

4. Bake 25 minutes or until lightly browned. Cool completely in pan on wire rack. Cut into bars. Reheat reserved caramel, if necessary; drizzle over bars.

Dulce de Leche Blondies

MINI KISSES® Blondies

Makes about 3 dozen blondies

½ cup (1 stick) butter or margarine, softened
1⅓ cups packed light brown sugar
2 eggs
2 teaspoons vanilla extract
¼ teaspoon salt

2 cups all-purpose flour
1½ teaspoons baking powder
1¾ cups (10-ounce package) HERSHEY'S MINI KISSES® Brand Milk Chocolates
½ cup chopped nuts

1. Heat oven to 350°F. Lightly grease 13×9-inch baking pan.

2. Beat butter and brown sugar in large bowl until fluffy. Add eggs, vanilla and salt; beat until blended. Add flour and baking powder; beat just until blended. Stir in chocolate pieces. Spread batter in prepared pan. Sprinkle nuts over top.

3. Bake 28 to 30 minutes or until set and golden brown. Cool completely in pan on wire rack. Cut into bars.

Maraschino Brownies

Makes 2 dozen brownies

1 (21-ounce) package brownie mix (13×9 pan size) plus ingredients to prepare mix

1 (8-ounce) container plain low-fat yogurt
1 (10-ounce) jar maraschino cherries, drained

Prepare brownie mix according to package directions, adding yogurt with liquid ingredients; mix well. Stir in cherries. Spoon batter into greased and floured 13×9×2-inch baking pan. Make sure cherries are evenly distributed.

Bake in preheated 350°F oven 28 to 30 minutes. Do not overbake. Brownies will be moist and cannot be tested with wooden pick.

Favorite recipe from **Cherry Marketing Institute**

MINI KISSES® Blondies

Peppermint Brownies
Makes about 1½ dozen brownies

4 squares (1 ounce each) unsweetened
    baking chocolate
½ cup (1 stick) unsalted butter, softened
2 cups sugar
4 eggs

1 cup all-purpose flour
½ teaspoon peppermint extract
1 cup coarsely chopped walnuts (optional)
½ cup finely crushed peppermint candies*

About 18 peppermint candies will yield ½ cup finely crushed peppermints. To crush, place unwrapped candy in a heavy-duty resealable food storage bag. Loosely seal the bag, leaving an opening for air to escape. Crush with a rolling pin, meat mallet or the bottom of a heavy skillet.

1. Preheat oven to 325°F. Grease 9-inch square baking pan.

2. Place chocolate and butter in medium microwavable bowl. Microwave on HIGH at 30-second intervals, stirring between each interval until melted and smooth.** Cool slightly.

3. Whisk sugar and eggs in large bowl until blended. Add chocolate mixture; mix well. Gradually add flour, stirring just until moistened. Fold in peppermint extract and walnuts, if desired. Spread batter in prepared pan.

4. Bake 35 minutes or until edges begin to pull away from sides of pan. Immediately sprinkle crushed candy over top. Cool completely in pan on wire rack. Cut into bars.

**Or combine chocolate and butter in top of double boiler over simmering water. Stir constantly until melted and smooth. Remove from heat immediately. Avoid getting any water in the chocolate or it will become brittle and hard.*

Peppermint Brownies

Mocha Fudge Brownies

Makes about 1 dozen brownies

3 squares (1 ounce each) semisweet
    chocolate

¾ cup sugar

½ cup (1 stick) butter, softened

2 eggs

2 teaspoons instant espresso powder

1 teaspoon vanilla

½ cup all-purpose flour

½ cup chopped almonds, toasted*

1 cup (6 ounces) milk chocolate chips,
    divided

To toast almonds, spread in single layer on baking sheet. Bake in preheated 350°F oven 8 to 10 minutes or until golden brown, stirring frequently.

1. Preheat oven to 350°F. Grease 8-inch square baking pan.

2. Melt semisweet chocolate in top of double boiler over simmering water. Remove from heat; cool slightly.

3. Beat sugar and butter in medium bowl with electric mixer at medium speed until light and fluffy. Add eggs, one at a time, beating well after each addition. Add chocolate, espresso powder and vanilla; beat until blended. Stir in flour, almonds and ½ cup chocolate chips. Spread batter in prepared pan.

4. Bake 25 minutes or until set. Sprinkle with remaining ½ cup chocolate chips. Let stand until melted; spread evenly over brownies. Cool completely in pan on wire rack. Cut into bars.

Tip

For easy removal, line the baking pan with foil and leave at least 2 inches hanging over each end. Use the foil to lift out the brownies, invert onto a cutting board and carefully remove the foil. Then cut into bars.

Mocha Fudge Brownies

White Chocolate & Almond Blondies

Makes about 1½ dozen blondies

12 ounces white chocolate, broken into
  pieces
1 cup (2 sticks) unsalted butter
3 eggs

¾ cup all-purpose flour
1 teaspoon vanilla
½ cup slivered almonds

1. Preheat oven to 325°F. Grease and flour 9-inch square pan.

2. Melt white chocolate and butter in large heavy saucepan over low heat, stirring constantly. (White chocolate may separate.) Immediately remove from heat when chocolate is melted.

3. Add eggs; beat with electric mixer at medium speed until smooth. Beat in flour and vanilla. Spread batter in prepared pan. Sprinkle almonds over top.

4. Bake 30 minutes or until set. Cool completely in pan on wire rack. Cut into bars.

Cherry Pie Blondies

Makes about 1½ dozen blondies

1½ cups sugar
1 cup (2 sticks) unsalted butter or
  margarine, softened
4 eggs

1 tablespoon lemon juice
2 cups all-purpose flour
1 can (21 ounces) cherry pie filling
  Powdered sugar

1. Preheat oven to 350°F. Grease 15×10-inch jelly-roll pan.

2. Beat sugar and butter in large bowl with electric mixer at medium speed until light and fluffy. Add eggs, one at a time, beating well after each addition. Beat in lemon juice. Gradually add flour; beat until well blended.

3. Spread batter in prepared pan. Top with cherry pie filling; spread evenly over batter.

4. Bake 30 minutes or until lightly browned. Cool completely in pan on wire rack. Sprinkle with powdered sugar just before serving. Cut into bars.

White Chocolate & Almond Blondies

Chocolate Brownies Deluxe
Makes about 2 dozen brownies

½ cup (1 stick) butter or margarine, softened
1 cup sugar
2 eggs
1 teaspoon vanilla extract
1¼ cups all-purpose flour

¼ cup HERSHEY'S Cocoa
¼ teaspoon baking soda
¾ cup HERSHEY'S Syrup
1 cup REESE'S® Peanut Butter Chips
Fudge Brownie Frosting (recipe follows)

1. Heat oven to 350°F. Grease 13×9-inch baking pan.

2. Beat butter, sugar, eggs and vanilla in large bowl until fluffy. Stir together flour, cocoa and baking soda; add alternately with syrup to butter mixture, beating well after each addition. Stir in peanut butter chips. Spread batter in prepared pan.

3. Bake 40 to 45 minutes or until brownies begin to pull away from sides of pan. Cool completely in pan on wire rack. Prepare Fudge Brownie Frosting; spread over brownies. Cut into bars.

Fudge Brownie Frosting
Makes about 1 cup frosting

3 tablespoons butter or margarine, softened
3 tablespoons HERSHEY'S Cocoa
1 cup powdered sugar

1 tablespoon milk
¾ teaspoon vanilla extract

Beat butter and cocoa in small bowl until well blended; gradually add powdered sugar alternately with combined milk and vanilla, beating until smooth and of spreading consistency. Add additional milk, ½ teaspoon at a time, if needed.

Chocolate Brownies Deluxe

Not-So-Sinful Brownies

Makes 2 dozen brownies

¼ cup vegetable oil

3 squares (1 ounce each) unsweetened
    chocolate

1¼ cups granulated sugar

½ cup applesauce

4 egg whites *or* 2 eggs, lightly beaten

1 teaspoon vanilla

1 cup QUAKER® Oats (quick or old
    fashioned, uncooked)

1 cup all-purpose flour

1 teaspoon baking powder

¼ teaspoon salt (optional)

1 tablespoon powdered sugar

1. Heat oven to 350°F. Spray bottom of 13×9-inch baking pan with nonstick cooking spray.

2. Heat oil and chocolate over low heat in large saucepan until chocolate is melted, stirring frequently. Remove from heat. Stir in granulated sugar and applesauce until sugar is dissolved. Stir in egg whites and vanilla until completely blended. Add combined oats, flour, baking powder and salt, if desired; mix well. Spread evenly into pan.

3. Bake 22 to 25 minutes or until edges begin to pull away from sides of pan. Cool completely in pan on wire rack. Cut into bars. Store tightly covered. Sprinkle with powdered sugar just before serving.

Tip

Always use the pan size specified in the recipe to ensure proper doneness. If using a glass baking dish instead of a metal baking pan, reduce oven temperature by 25°F.

Not-So-Sinful Brownies

Coconut Blondies
Makes 2 dozen blondies

2 cups all-purpose flour
1½ tablespoons baking powder
½ teaspoon salt
1⅔ cups packed brown sugar
1 cup chopped toasted pecans*

¾ cup flaked coconut, lightly packed
¾ cup (1½ sticks) unsalted butter, melted and cooled
2 eggs, lightly beaten
1 teaspoon vanilla

To toast pecans, spread in single layer on cookie sheet. Bake in preheated 350°F oven 8 to 10 minutes or until golden brown, stirring frequently. Cool completely.

1. Preheat oven to 350°F. Grease 13×9-inch baking pan.

2. Combine flour, baking powder and salt in large bowl. Add brown sugar, pecans and coconut; mix well. Make well in center of dry ingredients. Pour in butter, eggs and vanilla; stir just until moistened. Spread batter in prepared pan.

3. Bake 25 minutes or until toothpick inserted into center comes out clean. Cool completely in pan on wire rack. Cut into bars.

Coconut Blondies

Fruit & Pecan Brownies

Makes about 1 dozen brownies

2 squares (1 ounce each) unsweetened
    chocolate
1 cup sugar
½ cup (1 stick) unsalted butter, softened
2 eggs
1 teaspoon vanilla

½ cup all-purpose flour
1 cup chopped dried mixed fruit
1 cup coarsely chopped pecans, divided
1 cup (6 ounces) semisweet chocolate chips,
    divided

1. Preheat oven to 350°F. Grease 8-inch square pan.

2. Melt unsweetened chocolate in top of double boiler over simmering water. Remove from heat; cool slightly.

3. Beat sugar and butter in large bowl with electric mixer at medium speed until light and fluffy. Add eggs, one at a time, beating well after each addition. Beat in chocolate and vanilla. Stir in flour, dried fruit, ½ cup pecans and ½ cup chocolate chips. Spread batter evenly in prepared pan. Sprinkle with remaining ½ cup pecans and ½ cup chocolate chips.

4. Bake 25 to 30 minutes or until center is set. Cover with foil while still warm. Cool completely in pan on wire rack. Cut into bars.

Tip

Pecans can be stored in an airtight container up to 3 months in the refrigerator and up to 6 months in the freezer.

Fruit & Pecan Brownies

Mocha-Cinnamon Blondies
Makes 2 dozen blondies

1¾ cups sugar
1 cup (2 sticks) unsalted butter, melted
    and cooled
4 eggs
1 cup all-purpose flour

2 teaspoons instant coffee granules
1 teaspoon ground cinnamon
¼ teaspoon salt
1 cup chopped pecans
¾ cup semisweet chocolate chips

1. Preheat oven to 350°F. Grease 13×9-inch baking pan.

2. Beat sugar, butter and eggs in large bowl with electric mixer at medium speed until light and fluffy. Add flour, coffee granules, cinnamon and salt; beat at low speed until blended. Stir in pecans and chocolate chips. Spread batter in prepared pan.

3. Bake 30 minutes or until sides begin to pull away from pan. Cool completely in pan on wire rack. Cut into bars.

Tex-Mex Brownies
Makes about 1 dozen brownies

½ cup (1 stick) butter
2 squares (1 ounce each) unsweetened
    chocolate
½ to 1 teaspoon ground red pepper
2 eggs

1 cup sugar
½ cup all-purpose flour
1 teaspoon vanilla
1 cup (6 ounces) semisweet
    chocolate chips

1. Preheat oven to 325°F. Grease and flour 8-inch square pan. Melt butter and unsweetened chocolate in small heavy saucepan over low heat. Remove from heat. Stir in red pepper; cool.

2. Beat eggs in medium bowl with electric mixer at medium speed until pale yellow. Add sugar, beating until blended. Beat in chocolate mixture. Stir in flour and vanilla. Spread batter in prepared pan.

3. Bake 30 minutes or until set. Sprinkle chocolate chips over top. Let stand until melted; spread evenly over brownies. Cool completely in pan on wire rack. Cut into bars.

Mocha-Cinnamon Blondies

Chunky Caramel Nut Brownies

Makes 2 dozen brownies

¾ cup (1½ sticks) butter
4 squares (1 ounce each) unsweetened
   chocolate
2 cups sugar
4 eggs
1 cup all-purpose flour

1 package (14 ounces) caramels
¼ cup whipping cream
2 cups pecan halves or coarsely chopped
   pecans, divided
1 package (12 ounces) milk chocolate
   chunks or chips, divided

1. Preheat oven to 350°F. Grease 13×9-inch baking pan.

2. Place butter and chocolate in large microwavable bowl. Microwave on HIGH 1½ to 2 minutes or until melted and smooth. Stir in sugar. Add eggs, one at a time, whisking well after each addition. Stir in flour. Spread half of batter in prepared pan. Bake 20 minutes.

3. Meanwhile, combine caramels and cream in medium microwavable bowl. Microwave on HIGH 1½ to 2 minutes or until caramels begin to melt; stir until melted and smooth. Stir in 1 cup pecans.

4. Spread caramel mixture over partially baked brownie layer. Sprinkle with half of chocolate chunks. Pour remaining brownie batter over top; sprinkle with remaining 1 cup pecan halves and chocolate chunks.

5. Bake 25 minutes or until set. Cool completely in pan on wire rack. Cut into bars.

Chunky Caramel Nut Brownies

Chocolate Bliss Caramel Brownies

Makes 3 dozen brownies

4 squares BAKER'S® Unsweetened Baking
Chocolate

¾ cup (1½ sticks) butter or margarine

2 cups sugar

4 eggs

1 cup flour

1 cup chopped PLANTERS® Pecans or
Walnut Halves

25 KRAFT® Caramels (½ of 14-ounce bag)

2 tablespoons milk

1 package (12 ounces) BAKER'S®
Semi-Sweet Chocolate Chunks

PREHEAT oven to 350°F. Line 13×9-inch baking pan with foil, with ends extending over sides of pan. Grease foil.

PLACE chocolate squares and butter in large microwavable bowl. Microwave on HIGH 2 minutes or until butter is melted. Stir until chocolate is completely melted. Add sugar; mix well. Blend in eggs. Add flour; mix well. Stir in pecans. Spread into prepared pan.

BAKE 30 to 35 minutes or until toothpick inserted in center comes out with fudgy crumbs. DO NOT OVERBAKE.

MEANWHILE place caramels and milk in microwavable bowl. Microwave on HIGH 2 minutes, stirring after 1 minute. Stir until caramels are completely melted and mixture is well blended. Gently spread over brownie in pan; sprinkle with chocolate chunks. Cool in pan on wire rack. Using foil handles, lift brownies from pan. Cut into 36 squares. Store in tightly covered container at room temperature.

Tip: If using 13×9-inch glass baking dish, prepare as directed, reducing oven temperature to 325°F.

Prep Time: 20 minutes • **Bake Time:** 30 to 35 minutes

Chocolate Bliss Caramel Brownie

Cinnamon-Wheat Brownies

Makes about 1 dozen brownies

2 squares (1 ounce each) unsweetened chocolate
½ cup (1 stick) butter, softened
1 cup packed dark brown sugar
2 eggs
1 teaspoon ground cinnamon

1 teaspoon vanilla
¼ teaspoon baking powder
¼ teaspoon ground ginger
⅛ teaspoon ground cloves
1 cup coarsely chopped walnuts
½ cup whole wheat flour

1. Preheat oven to 350°F. Grease 8-inch square baking pan.

2. Melt chocolate in top of double boiler over simmering water. Remove from heat; cool slightly.

3. Beat butter, sugar, eggs and chocolate in large bowl with electric mixer at medium speed until light and smooth. Blend in cinnamon, vanilla, baking powder, ginger and cloves. Stir in walnuts and flour until well blended. Spread batter evenly in prepared pan.

4. Bake 25 minutes or until center is set. Cool completely in pan on wire rack. Cut into bars.

Tip

Cinnamon can vary in flavor depending on where it is grown. Some of the world's sweetest and strongest comes from China and Vietnam. Like most spices, ground cinnamon will lose its strength over time, so if yours has been in the cabinet for a while, taste it before using to make sure it is still flavorful.

Cinnamon-Wheat Brownies

Acknowledgments

The publisher would like to thank the companies and organizations listed below for the use of their recipes and photographs in this publication.

ACH Food Companies, Inc.

Cherry Marketing Institute

Cream of Wheat® Cereal

Dole Food Company, Inc.

Grapes from California

The Hershey Company

Kraft Foods Global, Inc.

Nestlé USA

North Dakota Wheat Commission

Ortega®, A Division of B&G Foods, Inc.

The Quaker® Oatmeal Kitchens

Unilever

Index

Metric Conversion Chart

VOLUME MEASUREMENTS (dry)

1/8 teaspoon = 0.5 mL
1/4 teaspoon = 1 mL
1/2 teaspoon = 2 mL
3/4 teaspoon = 4 mL
1 teaspoon = 5 mL
1 tablespoon = 15 mL
2 tablespoons = 30 mL
1/4 cup = 60 mL
1/3 cup = 75 mL
1/2 cup = 125 mL
2/3 cup = 150 mL
3/4 cup = 175 mL
1 cup = 250 mL
2 cups = 1 pint = 500 mL
3 cups = 750 mL
4 cups = 1 quart = 1 L

VOLUME MEASUREMENTS (fluid)

1 fluid ounce (2 tablespoons) = 30 mL
4 fluid ounces (1/2 cup) = 125 mL
8 fluid ounces (1 cup) = 250 mL
12 fluid ounces (1 1/2 cups) = 375 mL
16 fluid ounces (2 cups) = 500 mL

WEIGHTS (mass)

1/2 ounce = 15 g
1 ounce = 30 g
3 ounces = 90 g
4 ounces = 120 g
8 ounces = 225 g
10 ounces = 285 g
12 ounces = 360 g
16 ounces = 1 pound = 450 g

DIMENSIONS

1/16 inch = 2 mm
1/8 inch = 3 mm
1/4 inch = 6 mm
1/2 inch = 1.5 cm
3/4 inch = 2 cm
1 inch = 2.5 cm

OVEN TEMPERATURES

250°F = 120°C
275°F = 140°C
300°F = 150°C
325°F = 160°C
350°F = 180°C
375°F = 190°C
400°F = 200°C
425°F = 220°C
450°F = 230°C

BAKING PAN SIZES

Utensil	Size in Inches/Quarts	Metric Volume	Size in Centimeters
Baking or Cake Pan (square or rectangular)	8×8×2	2 L	20×20×5
	9×9×2	2.5 L	23×23×5
	12×8×2	3 L	30×20×5
	13×9×2	3.5 L	33×23×5
Loaf Pan	8×4×3	1.5 L	20×10×7
	9×5×3	2 L	23×13×7
Round Layer Cake Pan	8×1½	1.2 L	20×4
	9×1½	1.5 L	23×4
Pie Plate	8×1¼	750 mL	20×3
	9×1¼	1 L	23×3
Baking Dish or Casserole	1 quart	1 L	—
	1½ quart	1.5 L	—
	2 quart	2 L	—